Fundamentals of Data Science

Dr. Monika G.
Head of the department & Assistant Professor
Department of Computer Science and Applications,
Jeppiaar College of Arts and Science,
Padur, Chennai.

Ms. D. Deepa
Assistant professor (SRG)
Department of Computer Science and Engineering,
Kongu Engineering College,
TamilNadu.

Dr. Pandimurugan
Assistant Professor,
Department of Computer Science and Engineering,
SRM Institute,
Chennai, Tamil Nadu.

978-1-716-54070-7

i

First Edition: March – 2023

Lulu Publisher

ISBN: 978-1-716-54070-7

AUTHOR PROFILE

**Dr. Monika G** *was Currently working as HOD i/c and Assistant Professor in Department of Computer science and applications at Jeppiaar College of arts and Science, she is also IPR Coordinator of college, EDC/IIC member, Research cell coordinator of department, Placement coordinator, admission cell coordinator, and Selection committee panel member. awarded PhD in Computer science from Vels Institute of Science Technology and advanced studies, Palavaram, Chennai in October 2021. She has done her Master of Science in Computer science in the year 2013 and Bachelor of science in computer science in the year 2011 from University of Madras. She has over 9 years of Research experience and teaching experience in different institutions. She has presented seven research articles in international conference. She has also published four journal papers in Scopus indexed and National journals. Recently she has published a book titled "Java and data structures". She has filed the patent in Intellectual Property Rights on "Anamoly Intrusion detection system to detect DDoS attack in private cloud environment". She is not only a academician, she was also practising Heartfulness meditation over 10 years. Her research interest was widely on Artificial Intelligence, Machine Learning, Educational Data mining and Cloud Computing.*

CONTENTS

Chapter I

Data Scientist

Chapter II

Introduction to Data

Chapter III

Level of Data Science

Chapter IV

Fundamentals of Mathematics

Chapter V

Machine Learning Essentials

Chapter VI

Predictions

PREFACE

The topic of this book is data science, which is a field of study and application that has been growing rapidly for the past several decades. As a growing field, it is gaining a lot of attention in both the media as well as in the job market. This move was modeled after tech companies who, honestly, only recently started hiring massive data teams. These skills are in high demand and their applications extend much further than today's job market. This book will attempt to bridge the gap between math/programming/domain expertises. Most people today have expertise in at least one of these (maybe two), but proper data science requires a little bit of all three. We will dive into topics from all three areas and solve complex problems. We will clean, explore, and analyze data in order to derive scientific and accurate conclusions. Machine learning and deep learning techniques will be applied to solve complex data tasks.

Authors

Chapter I
Data Scientist

1.1 What is data science

Before we go any further, let's look at some basic definitions that we will use throughout this book. The great/awful thing about this field is that it is so young that these definitions can differ from textbook to newspaper to whitepaper.

Basic terminology

The definitions that follow are general enough to be used in daily conversations and work to serve the purpose of the book, an introduction to the principles of data science.

Let's start by defining what data is. This might seem like a silly first definition to have, but it is very important. Whenever we use the word "data", we refer to a collection of information in either an organized or unorganized format:

- Organized data: This refers to data that is sorted into a row/column structure, where every row represents a single observation and the columns represent the characteristics of that observation.

- Unorganized data: This is the type of data that is in the free form, usually text or raw audio/signals that must be parsed further to become organized. Whenever you open Excel (or any other spreadsheet program), you are looking at a blank row/column structure waiting for organized data. These programs don't do well with unorganized data. For the most part, we will deal with organized data as it is the easiest to glean insight from, but we will not shy away from looking at raw text and methods of processing unorganized forms of data.

Data science is the art and science of acquiring knowledge through data. What a small definition for such a big topic, and rightfully so! Data science covers so many things that it would take pages to list it all out (I should know, I tried and got edited down).

Data science is all about how we take data, use it to acquire knowledge, and then use that knowledge to do the following:
- Make decisions
- Predict the future
- Understand the past/present
- Create new industries/products

This book is all about the methods of data science, including how to process data, gather insights, and use those insights to make informed decisions and predictions.

Data science is about using data in order to gain new insights that you would Otherwise have missed. As an example, imagine you are sitting around a table with three other people. The four of you have to make a decision based on some data. There are four opinions to consider. You would use data science to bring a fifth, sixth, and even seventh opinion to the table. That's why data science won't replace the human brain, but complements it, work alongside it. Data science should not be thought of as an end-all solution to our data woes; it is merely an opinion, a very informed opinion, but an opinion nonetheless. It deserves a seat at the table.

1.2 The data science diagram

It is a common misconception that only those with a PhD or geniuses can understand the math/programming behind data science.

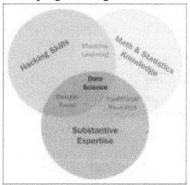

The Venn diagram of data science

This is absolutely false. Understanding data science begins with three basic areas:
- Math/statistics: This is the use of equations and formulas to perform analysis
- Computer programming: This is the ability to use code to create outcomes on the computer
- Domain knowledge: This refers to understanding the problem domain (medicine, finance, social science, and so on)

The following Venn diagram provides a visual representation of how the three areas of data science intersect:

Those with hacking skills can conceptualize and program complicated algorithms using computer languages. Having a Math & Statistics Knowledge base allows you to theorize and evaluate algorithms and tweak the existing procedures to fit specific situations. Having Substantive Expertise (domain expertise) allows you to apply concepts and results in a meaningful and effective way. While having only two of these three qualities can make you intelligent, it will also leave a gap. Consider that you are very skilled in coding and have formal training in day trading. You might create an automated system to trade in your place but lack the math skills to evaluate your algorithms and, therefore, end up losing money in the long run. It is only when you can boast skills in coding, math, and domain knowledge that you can truly perform data science.

The one that was probably a surprise for you was Domain Knowledge. It is really just knowledge of the area you are working in. If a financial analyst started analyzing data about heart attacks, they might need the help of a cardiologist to make sense of a lot of the numbers.

Data Science is the intersection of the three key areas mentioned earlier. In order to gain knowledge from data, we must be able to utilize computer programming to access the data, understand the mathematics behind the models we derive, and above all, understand our analyses' place in the domain we are in. This includes the presentation of data. If we are creating a model to predict heart attacks in patients, is it better to create a PDF of information or an app where you can type in numbers and get a quick prediction? All these decisions must be made by the data scientist.

Both computer programming and math are covered extensively in this book. Domain knowledge comes with both practice of data science and reading examples of other people's analyses.

The math

Most people stop listening once someone says the word math. They'll nod along in an attempt to hide their utter disdain for the topic. This book will guide you through the math needed for data science, specifically statistics and probability. We will use these subdomains of mathematics to create what are called models.

A data model refers to an organized and formal relationship between elements of data, usually meant to simulate a real-world phenomenon. Essentially, we will use math in order to formalize relationships between variables. As a former pure mathematician and current math teacher, I know how difficult this can be. I will do my best to explain everything as clearly as I can. Between the three areas of data science, math is what allows us to move from domain to domain.

Understanding the theory allows us to apply a model that we built for the fashion industry to a financial model. The math covered in this book ranges from basic algebra to advanced probabilistic and statistical modeling. Do not skip over these chapters, even if you already know it or you're afraid of it. Every mathematical concept I introduce, I do so with care, examples, and purpose. The math in this book is essential for data scientists.

1.3 Terminology

This is a good time to define some more vocabulary. By this point, you're probably excitedly looking up a lot of data science material and seeing words and phrases I haven't used yet. Here are some common terminologies you are likely to come across:

- **Machine learning:** This refers to giving computers the ability to learn from data without explicit "rules" being given by a programmer. We have seen the concept of machine learning earlier in this chapter as the union of someone who has both coding and math skills. Here, we are attempting to formalize this definition. Machine learning combines the power of computers with intelligent learning algorithms in order to automate the discovery of relationships in data and create of powerful data models. Speaking of data models, we will concern ourselves with the following two basic types of data models:
- **Probabilistic model:** This refers to using probability to find a relationship between elements that includes a degree of randomness.
- **Statistical model:** This refers to taking advantage of statistical theorems to formalize relationships between data elements in a (usually) simple mathematical formula.

While both the statistical and probabilistic models can be run on computers and might be considered machine learning in that regard, we will keep these definitions separate as machine learning algorithms generally attempt to learn relationships in different ways.

We will take a look at the statistical and probabilistic models in the later chapters.

- **Exploratory data analysis (EDA)** refers to preparing data in order to standardize results and gain quick insights. EDA is concerned with data visualization and preparation. This is where we turn unorganized data into organized data and also clean up missing/ incorrect data points. During EDA, we will create many types of plots and use these plots to identify key features and relationships to exploit in our data models.
- **Data mining** is the process of finding relationships between elements of data. Data mining is the part of data science where we try to find relationships between variables (think spawn-recruit model).

I tried pretty hard not to use the term big data up until now. This is because I think this term is misused, a lot. While the definition of this word varies from person, big data. Big Data is data that is too large to be processed by a single machine (if your laptop crashed, it might be suffering from a case of big data).

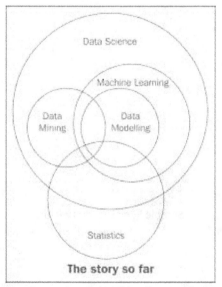

The state of data science (so far). This diagram is incomplete and is meant for visualization purposes only.

1.4 Data science case studies

The combination of math, computer programming, and domain knowledge is what makes data science so powerful. Often, it is difficult for a single person to master all three of these areas. That's why it's very common for companies to hire teams of data scientists instead of a single person. Let's look at a few powerful examples of data science in action and their outcome.

Case study – automating government paper pushing

Social security claims are known to be a major hassle for both the agent reading it and for the person who wrote the claim. Some claims take over 2 years to get resolved in their entirety, and that's absurd! Let's look at what goes into a claim:

Sample social security form

Not bad. It's mostly just text, though. Fill this in, then that, then this, and so on. You can see how it would be difficult for an agent to read these all day, form after form.

There must be a better way! Well, there is. Elder Research Inc. parsed this unorganized data and was able to automate 20% of all disability social security forms. This means that a computer could look at 20% of these written forms and give its opinion on the approval.

Not only that, the third-party company that is hired to rate the approvals of the forms actually gave the machine-graded forms a higher grade than the human forms. So, not only did the computer handle 20% of the load, it, on average, did better than a human.

A dataset shows the relationship between the money spent in the categories of TV, radio, and newspaper. The goal is to analyze the relationship between the three different marketing mediums and how it affects the sale of a product. Our data is in the form of a row and column structure. Each row represents a sales region and the columns tell us how much money was spent on each medium and the profit achieved in that region.

	TV	Radio	Newspaper	Sales
1	230.1	37.8	69.2	22.1
2	44.5	39.3	45.1	10.4
3	17.2	45.9	69.3	9.3
4	151.5	41.3	58.5	18.5
5	180.8	10.8	58.4	12.9

Advertising budgets

For example, in the third region, we spent $17,200 on TV advertising and sold 9,300 widgets.

If we plot each variable against sales, we get the following graphs:

import seaborn as sns
sns.pairplot(data, x_vars=['TV','Radio','Newspaper'], y_vars='Sales')

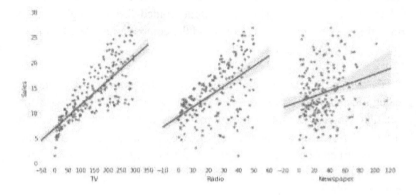

Graphs of advertising budgets

Note how none of these variables form a very strong line and, therefore, might not work well to predict sales (on their own). TV comes closest in forming an obvious relationship, but still even that isn't great. In this case, we will have to form a more complex model than the one we used in the spawner-recruiter model and combine all three variables in order to model sales.

Case study – what's in a job description?

Looking for a job in data science? Great, let me help. In this case study, I have "scraped" (taken from the Web) 1,000 job descriptions for companies actively hiring data scientists (as of January 2016). The goal here is to look at some of the most common keywords people use in their job descriptions.

Machine Learning Quantitative Analyst
Bloomberg - ★★★★★ 282 reviews - New York, NY
The Machine Learning Quantitative Analyst will work in Bloomberg's Enterprise Solutions area and work collaboratively to build a liquidity tool for banks...
8 days ago - email
Sponsored

Save lives with machine learning
Blue Owl - San Francisco, CA
Requirements for all data scientists. Expert in Python and core libraries used by data scientists (Numpy, Scipy, Pandas, Scikit-learn, Matplotlib/Seaborn, etc.)...
36+ days ago - email
Sponsored

Data Scientist
Indeed - ★★★★★ 132 reviews - Austin, TX
How a Data Scientist works. As a Data Scientist at Indeed your role is to follow the data. We are looking for a mixture between a statistician, scientist,...
Easily apply
30+ days ago - email
Sponsored

An example of data scientist job listings.

import requests
 # used to grab data from the web

from BeautifulSoup import BeautifulSoup
 # used to parse HTML

from sklearn.feature_extraction.text import CountVectorizer
 # used to count number of words and phrases (we will be using this module a lot)

Notable things:

- Machine learning and experience are at the top of the list. Experience comes with practice. A basic idea of machine learning comes with this book.
- These words are followed closely by statistical words implying knowledge of math and theory.
- The word team is very high up, implying that you will need to work with a team of data scientists; you won't be a lone wolf.
- Computer science words such as algorithms and programming are prevalent.

- The words techniques, understanding, and methods imply a more theoretical approach, ambivalent to any single domain.
- The word business implies a particular problem domain.

There are many interesting things to note about this case study but the biggest take away is that there are many key words and phrases that make up a data science role. It isn't just math, coding, or domain knowledge; it truly is the combination of these three ideas (whether exemplified in a single person or across a multiperson team) that makes data science possible and powerful.

Chapter II
Introduction to Data

2.1 Data: Structured versus unstructured

The distinction between structured and unstructured data is usually the first question you want to ask yourself about the entire dataset. The answer to this question can mean the difference between needing three days or three weeks of time to perform a proper analysis.

The basic breakdown is as follows (this is a rehashed definition of organized and unorganized data in the first chapter):
- Structured (organized) data: This is data that can be thought of as observations and characteristics. It is usually organized using a table method (rows and columns).
- Unstructured (unorganized) data: This data exists as a free entity and does not follow any standard organization hierarchy.

Here are a few examples that could help you differentiate between the two:
- Most data that exists in text form, including server logs and Facebook posts, is unstructured
- Scientific observations, as recorded by careful scientists, are kept in a very neat and organized (structured) format
- A genetic sequence of chemical nucleotides (for example, ACGTATTGCA) is unstructured even if the order of the nucleotides matters as we cannot form descriptors of the sequence using a row/column format without taking a further look.

Structured data is generally thought of as being much easier to work with and analyze. Most statistical and machine learning models were built with structured data in mind and cannot work on the loose interpretation of unstructured data. The natural row and column structure is easy to digest for human and machine eyes. So why even talk about unstructured data? Because it is so common! Most estimates place unstructured data as 80-90% of the world's data. This data exists in many forms and for the most part, goes unnoticed by humans as a potential source of data. Tweets, e-mails, literature, and server logs are generally unstructured forms of data. While a data scientist likely prefers structured data, they must be able to deal with the world's massive amounts of unstructured data. If 90% of the world's data is unstructured, that implies that about 90% of the world's information is trapped in a difficult format.

So, with most of our data existing in this free-form format, we must turn to preanalysis techniques, called preprocessing, in order to apply structure to at least a part of the data for further analysis. The next chapter will deal with preprocessing in great detail; for now, we will consider the part of preprocessing wherein we attempt to apply transformations to convert unstructured data into a structured counterpart.

Example of data preprocessing

When looking at text data (which is almost always considered unstructured), we have many options to transform the set into a structured format. We may do this by applying new characteristics that describe the data. A few such characteristics are as follows:
- Word/phrase count
- The existence of certain special characters
- The relative length of text
- Picking out topics

I will use the following tweet as a quick example of unstructured data, but you may use any unstructured free-form text that you like, including tweets and Facebook posts.
This Wednesday morn, are you early to rise? Then look East. The Crescent Moon joins Venus & Saturn. Afloat in the dawn skies. It is important to reiterate that pre-processing is necessary for this tweet because a vast majority of learning algorithms require numerical data (which we will get into after this example).

13

More than requiring a certain type of data, pre-processing allows us to explore features that have been created from the existing features. For example, we can extract features such as word count and special characters from the mentioned tweet. Now, let's take a look at a few features that we can extract from text.

Word/phrase counts

We may break down a tweet into its word/phrase count. The word this appears in the tweet once, as does every other word. We can represent this tweet in a structured format, as follows, thereby converting the unstructured set of words into a row/column format:

	this	wednesday	morn	are	this wednesday
Word Count	1	1	1	1	1

Presence of certain special characters

We may also look at the presence of special characters, such as the question mark and exclamation mark. The appearance of these characters might imply certain ideas about the data that are otherwise difficult to know. For example, the fact that this tweet contains a question mark might strongly imply that this tweet contains a question for the reader. We might append the preceding table with a new column, as shown:

	this	wednesday	morn	are	this wednesday	?
Word Count	1	1	1	1	1	1

Relative length of text

This tweet is 121 characters long.

len("This Wednesday morn, are you early to rise? Then look East. The Crescent Moon joins Venus & Saturn. Afloat in the dawn skies.")
 # get the length of this text (number of characters for a string)

14

The average tweet, as discovered by analysts, is about 30 characters in length. So, we might impose a new characteristic, called relative length, (which is the length of the tweet divided by the average length), telling us the length of this tweet as compared to the average tweet. This tweet is actually 4.03 times longer than the average tweet, as shown:
We can add yet another column to our table using this method:

	this	wednesday	morn	are	this wednesday	?	Relative length
Word Count	1	1	1	1	1	1	4.03

Picking out topics

We can pick out some topics of the tweet to add as columns. This tweet is about astronomy, so we can add another column, as illustrated:

	this	wednesday	morn	are	this wednesday	?	Relative length	Topic
Word Count	1	1	1	1	1	1	4.03	astronomy

And just like that, we can convert a piece of text into structured/organized data ready for use in our models and exploratory analysis.

Topic is the only extracted feature we looked at that is not automatically derivable from the tweet. Looking at word count and tweet length in Python is easy; however, more advanced models (called topic models) are able to derive and predict topics of natural text as well.

Being able to quickly recognize whether your data is structured or unstructured can save hours or even days of work in the future. Once you are able to discern the organization of the data presented to you, the next question is aimed at the individual characteristics of the dataset.

2.2 Quantitative versus qualitative

When you ask a data scientist, "what type of data is this?", they will usually assume that you are asking them whether or not it is mostly quantitative or qualitative. It is likely the most common way of describing the specific characteristics of a dataset. For the most part, when talking about quantitative data, you are usually (not always) talking about a structured dataset with a strict row/column structure (because we don't assume unstructured data even has any characteristics). All the more reason why the preprocessing step is so important.

These two data types can be defined as follows:

- Quantitative data: This data can be described using numbers, and basic mathematical procedures, including addition, are possible on the set.

- Qualitative data: This data cannot be described using numbers and basic mathematics. This data is generally thought of as being described using "natural" categories and language.

Example – coffee shop data

Say that we were processing observations of coffee shops in a major city using the following five descriptors (characteristics):

Data: Coffee Shop

- Name of coffee shop
- Revenue (in thousands of dollars)
- Zip code
- Average monthly customers
- Country of coffee origin

Each of these characteristics can be classified as either quantitative or qualitative, and that simple distinction can change everything. Let's take a look at each one:

- Name of coffee shop – Qualitative
  The name of a coffee shop is not expressed as a number and we cannot perform math on the name of the shop.

- Revenue – Quantitative
  How much money a cafe brings in can definitely be described using a number. Also, we can do basic operations such as adding up the revenue for 12 months to get a year's worth of revenue.

- Zip code – Qualitative
  This one is tricky. A zip code is always represented using numbers, but what makes it qualitative is that it does not fit the second part of the definition of quantitative—we cannot perform basic mathematical operations on a zip code. If we add together two zip codes, it is a nonsensical measurement. We don't necessarily get a new zip code and we definitely don't get "double the zip code".

- Average monthly customers – Quantitative
  Again, describing this factor using numbers and addition makes sense. Add up all of your monthly customers and you get your yearly customers.

- Country of coffee origin – Qualitative
  We will assume this is a very small café with coffee from a single origin. This country is described using a name (Ethiopian, Colombian), and not numbers.

2.3 Levels of data

It is generally understood that a specific characteristic (feature/column) of structured data can be broken down into one of four levels of data. The levels are:

- The nominal level
- The ordinal level
- The interval level
- The ratio level

As we move down the list, we gain more structure and, therefore, more returns from our analysis. Each level comes with its own accepted practice in measuring the center of the data. We usually think of the mean/average as being an acceptable form of center, however, this is only true for a specific type of data.

The nominal level

The first level of data, the nominal level, (which also sounds like the word name) consists of data that is described purely by name or category. Basic examples include gender, nationality, species, or yeast strain in a beer. They are not described by numbers and are therefore qualitative. The following are some examples:

- A type of animal is on the nominal level of data. We may also say that if you are a chimpanzee, then you belong to the mammalian class as well.
- A part of speech is also considered on the nominal level of data. The word she is a pronoun, and it is also a noun.

Of course, being qualitative, we cannot perform any quantitative mathematical operations, such as addition or division. These would not make any sense.

Mathematical operations allowed

We cannot perform mathematics on the nominal level of data except the basic equality and set membership functions, as shown in the following two examples:
• Being a tech entrepreneur is the same as being in the tech industry, but not vice versa
• A figure described as a square falls under the description of being a rectangle, but not vice versa

Measures of center

A measure of center is a number that describes what the data tends to. It is sometimes referred to as the balance point of the data. Common examples include the mean, median, and mode.

In order to find the center of nominal data, we generally turn to the mode (the most common element) of the dataset. For example, look back at the WHO alcohol consumption data. The most common continent surveyed was Africa, making that a possible choice for the center of the continent column.

Measures of center such as the mean and median do not make sense at this level as we cannot order the observations or even add them together.

What data is like at the nominal level

Data at the nominal level is mostly categorical in nature. Because we generally can only use words to describe the data, it can be lost in translation among countries, or can even be misspelled.

While data at this level can certainly be useful, we must be careful about what insights we may draw from them. With only the mode as a basic measure of center, we are unable to draw conclusions about an average observation. This concept does not exist at this level. It is only at the next level that we may begin to perform true mathematics on our observations.

The ordinal level

The nominal level did not provide us with much flexibility in terms of mathematical operations due to one seemingly unimportant fact—we could not order the observations in any natural way. Data in the ordinal level provides us with a rank order, or the means to place one observation before the other; however, it does not provide us with relative differences between observations, meaning that while we may order the observations from first to last, we cannot add or subtract them to get any real meaning.

Examples

The Likert is among the most common ordinal level scales. Whenever you are given a survey asking you to rate your satisfaction on a scale from 1 to 10, you are providing data at the ordinal level. Your answer, which must fall between 1 and 10, can be ordered: eight is better than seven while three is worse than nine.

However, differences between the numbers do not make much sense. The difference between a seven and a six might be different than the difference between a two and a one.

Mathematical operations allowed

We are allowed much more freedom on this level in mathematical operations. We inherit all mathematics from the ordinal level (equality and set membership) and we can also add the following to the list of operations allowed in the nominal level:

- Ordering
- Comparison

Ordering refers to the natural order provided to us by the data; however, this can be tricky to figure out sometimes. When speaking about the spectrum of visible light, we can refer to the names of colors—red, orange, yellow, green, blue, indigo, and violet. Naturally, as we move from left to right, the light is gaining energy and other properties. We may refer to this as a natural order.

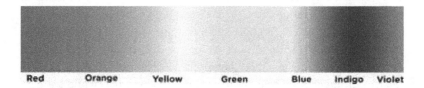

However, if needed, an artist may impose another order on the data, such as sorting the colors based on the cost of the material to make the said color. This could change the order of the data but as long as we are consistent in what defines the order, it does not matter what defines it.

Comparisons are another new operation allowed at this level. At the ordinal level, it would not make sense to say that one country was naturally better than another or that one part of speech is worse than another. At the ordinal level, we can make these comparisons. For example, we can talk about how putting a "7" on a survey is worse than putting a "10".

Measures of center

At the ordinal level, the median is usually an appropriate way of defining the center of the data. The mean, however, would be impossible because division is not allowed at this level. We can also use the mode like we could at the nominal level.

We will now look at an example of using the median:

Imagine you have conducted a survey among your employees asking "how happy are you to be working here on a scale from 1-5", and your results are as follows
:
5, 4, 3, 4, 5, 3, 2, 5, 3, 2, 1, 4, 5, 3, 4, 4, 5, 4, 2, 1, 4, 5, 4, 3, 2, 4, 4, 5, 4, 3, 2, 1

Let's use Python to find the median of this data. It is worth noting that most people would argue that the mean of these scores would work just fine. The reason that the mean would not be as mathematically viable is because if we subtract/add two scores, say a score of four minus a score of two, the difference of two does not really mean anything. If addition/subtraction among the scores doesn't make sense, the mean won't make sense either.

```
import numpy
results = [5, 4, 3, 4, 5, 3, 2, 5, 3, 2, 1, 4, 5, 3, 4, 4, 5, 4, 2, 1,
4, 5, 4, 3, 2, 4, 4, 5, 4, 3, 2, 1]

sorted_results = sorted(results)

print sorted_results
'''
[1, 1, 1, 2, 2, 2, 2, 2, 3, 3, 3, 3, 3, 3, 4, 4, 4, 4, 4, 4, 4, 4, 4,
4, 4, 5, 5, 5, 5, 5, 5, 5]
'''
print numpy.mean(results) # == 3.4375
print numpy.median(results) # == 4.0
```

Turns out that the median is not only more sound, but makes the survey results look much better.

The interval level

Now we are getting somewhere interesting. At the interval level, we are beginning to look at data that can be expressed through very quantifiable means, and where much more complicated mathematical formulas are allowed. The basic difference between the ordinal level and the interval level is, well, just that—difference.

Data at the interval level allows meaningful subtraction between data points.

Example

Temperature is a great example of data at the interval level. If it is 100 degrees
Fahrenheit in Texas and 80 degrees Fahrenheit in Istanbul, Turkey, then Texas is 20 degrees warmer than Istanbul. This simple example allows for so much more manipulation at this level than previous examples.

Measures of center

At this level, we can use the median and mode to describe this data; however, usually the most accurate description of the center of data would be the arithmetic mean, more commonly referred to as, simply, "the mean". Recall that the definition of the mean requires us to add together all the measurements. At the previous levels, addition was meaningless; therefore, the mean would have lost extreme value. It is only at the interval level and above that the arithmetic mean makes sense.

We will now look at an example of using the mean.

Suppose we look at the temperature of a fridge containing a pharmaceutical company's new vaccine. We measure the temperate every hour with the following data points (in Fahrenheit):

31, 32, 32, 31, 28, 29, 31, 38, 32, 31, 30, 29, 30, 31, 26

Using Python again, let's find the mean and median of the data:

```
import numpy
temps = [31, 32, 32, 31, 28, 29, 31, 38, 32, 31, 30, 29, 30, 31, 26]

print numpy.mean(temps) # == 30.73
print numpy.median(temps) # == 31.0
```

Measures of variation

This is something new that we have not yet discussed. It is one thing to talk about the center of the data but, in data science, it is also very important to mention how "spread out" the data is. The measures that describe this phenomenon are called measures of variation. You have likely heard of "standard deviation" before and are now experiencing mild PTSD from your statistics classes. This idea is extremely important and I would like to address it briefly.

A measure of variation (like the standard deviation) is a number that attempts to describe how spread out the data is.

Along with a measure of center, a measure of variation can almost entirely describe a dataset with only two numbers.

Standard deviation

Arguably, standard deviation is the most common measure of variation of data at the interval level and beyond. The standard deviation can be thought of as the "average distance a data point is at from the mean". While this description is technically and mathematically incorrect, it is a good way to think about it. The formula for standard deviation can be broken down into the following steps:

- Find the mean of the data.
- For each number in the dataset, subtract it from the mean and then square it.
- Find the average of each square difference.
- Take the square root of the number obtained in step three. This is the standard deviation.

Notice how, in the steps, we do actually take an arithmetic mean as one of the steps.

The ratio level

Finally, we will take a look at the ratio level. After moving through three different levels with differing levels of allowed mathematical operations, the ratio level proves to be the strongest of the four.

24

Not only can we define order and difference, the ratio level allows us to multiply and divide as well. This might seem like not much to make a fuss over but it changes almost everything about the way we view data at this level.

Examples

While Fahrenheit and Celsius are stuck in the interval level, the Kelvin scale of temperature boasts a natural zero. A measurement zero Kelvin literally means the absence of heat. It is a non-arbitrary starting zero. We can actually scientifically say that 200 Kelvin is twice as much heat as 100 Kelvin.

Money in the bank is at the ratio level. You can have "no money in the bank" and it makes sense that $200,000 is "twice as much as" $100,000.

2.4 Data beholder

It is possible to impose structure on data. For example, while I said that you technically cannot use a mean for the one to five data at the ordinal scale, many statisticians would not have a problem using this number as a descriptor of the dataset.

The level at which you are interpreting data is a huge assumption that should be made at the beginning of any analysis. If you are looking at data that is generally thought of at the ordinal level and applying tools such as the arithmetic mean and standard deviation, this is something that data scientists must be aware of. This is mainly because if you continue to hold these assumptions as valid in your analysis, you may encounter problems. For example, if you also assume divisibility at the ordinal level by mistake, you are imposing structure where structure may not exist.

Chapter III
Level of Data Science

3.1 Introduction to Data Science

Many people ask me the biggest difference between data science and data analytics. While one can argue that there is no difference between the two, many will argue that there are hundreds! I believe that regardless of how many differences there are between the two terms, the biggest is that data science follows a structured, step-by-step process that, when followed, preserves the integrity of the results.

Like any other scientific endeavor, this process must be adhered to, or else the analysis and the results are in danger of scrutiny. On a simpler level, following a strict process can make it much easier for amateur data scientists to obtain results faster than if they were exploring data with no clear vision.

While these steps are a guiding lesson for amateur analysts, they also provide the foundation for all data scientists, even those in the highest levels of business and academia. Every data scientist recognizes the value of these steps and follows them in some way or another.

3.2 Overview of the levels
The five essential steps to perform data science are as follows:
- Asking an interesting question
- Obtaining the data
- Exploring the data
- Modeling the data
- Communicating and visualizing the results

First, let's look at the five steps with reference to the big picture.

Ask an interesting question

This is probably my favorite step. As an entrepreneur, I ask myself (and others) interesting questions every day. I would treat this step as you would treat a brainstorming session. Start writing down questions regardless of whether or not you think the data to answer these questions even exists. The reason for this is twofold. First off, you don't want to start biasing yourself even before searching for data. Secondly, obtaining data might involve searching in both public and private locations and, therefore, might not be very straightforward. You might ask a question and immediately tell yourself "Oh, but I bet there's no data out there that can help me," and cross it off your list. Don't do that! Leave it on your list.

Obtain the data

Once you have selected the question you want to focus on, it is time to scour the world for the data that might be able to answer that question. As mentioned before, the data can come from a variety of sources; so, this step can be very creative!

Explore the data

Once we have the data, we use the lessons learned in Chapter 2, Types of Data, of this book and begin to break down the types of data that we are dealing with. This is a pivotal step in the process. Once this step is completed, the analyst generally has spent several hours learning about the domain, using code or other tools to manipulate and explore the data, and has a very good sense of what the data might be trying to tell them.

Model the data

This step involves the use of statistical and machine learning models. In this step, we are not only fitting and choosing models, we are implanting mathematical validation metrics in order to quantify the models and their effectiveness.

Communicate and visualize the results

This is arguably the most important step. While it might seem obvious and simple, the ability to conclude your results in a digestible format is much more difficult than it seems. We will look at different examples of cases when results were communicated poorly and when they were displayed very well.

3.3 Explore the data

The process of exploring data is not defined simply. It involves the ability to recognize the different types of data, transform data types, and use code to systemically improve the quality of the entire dataset to prepare it for the modeling stage. In order to best represent and teach the art of exploration, I will present several different datasets and use the python package pandas to explore the data. Along the way, we will run into different tips and tricks for how to handle data.

There are three basic questions we should ask ourselves when dealing with a new dataset that we may not have seen before. Keep in mind that these questions are not the beginning and the end of data science; they are some guidelines that should be followed when exploring a newly obtained set of data.

Basic questions for data exploration

When looking at a new dataset, whether it is familiar to you or not, it is important to use the following questions as guidelines for your preliminary analysis:

- Is the data organized or not?
  We are checking for whether or not the data is presented in a row/column structure. For the most part, data will be presented in an organized fashion. In this book, over 90% of our examples will begin with organized data. Nevertheless, this is the most basic question that we can answer before diving any deeper into our analysis.

  A general rule of thumb is that if we have unorganized data, we want to transform it into a row/column structure. For example, earlier in this book, we looked at ways to transform text into a row/column structure by counting the number of words/phrases.

- What does each row represent?
  Once we have an answer to how the data is organized and are now lookingat a nice row/column based dataset, we should identify what each row actually represents. This step is usually very quick, and can help put things in perspective much more quickly.

- What does each column represent?
  We should identify each column by the level of data and whether or not it is quantitative/qualitative, and so on. This categorization might change as our analysis progresses, but it is important to begin this step as early as possible.

- Are there any missing data points?
  Data isn't perfect. Sometimes we might be missing data because of human or mechanical error. When this happens, we, as data scientists, must make decisions about how to deal with these discrepancies.

- Do we need to perform any transformations on the columns?
  Depending on what level/type of data each column is at, we might need to perform certain types of transformations. For example, generally speaking, for the sake of statistical modeling and machine learning, we would like each column to be numerical. Of course, we will use Python to make any and all transformations.

All the while, we are asking ourselves the overall question, what can we infer from the preliminary inferential statistics? We want to be able to understand our data a bit more than when we first found it.

Enough talk, let's see an example in the following section.

Dataset 1 – Yelp

The first dataset we will look at is a public dataset made available by the restaurant review site, Yelp. All personally identifiable information has been removed. Let's read in the data first, as shown here:

```
import pandas as pd
yelp_raw_data = pd.read_csv("yelp.csv")
yelp_raw_data.head()
```

A quick recap of what the preceding code does:
- Import the pandas package and nickname it as pd.
- Read in the .csv from the Web; call is yelp_raw_data.
- Look at the head of the data (just the first few rows).

business_id	date	review_id	stars	text	type	user_id	cool	useful	funny
0	2011-01-26			My wife took me here on my birthday for breakf...	review		2	5	0
1	2011-07-27			I have no idea why some people give bad revie...	review		0	0	0
2	2012-06-14			love the gyro plate. Rice is so good and I als...	review		0	1	0
3	2010-05-27			Rosie, Dakota, and I LOVE Chaparral Dog Park!...	review		1	2	0
4	2012-01-05			General Manager Scott Petello is a good egg!!...	review		0	0	0

Is the data organized or not?

• Because we have a nice row/column structure, we can conclude that this data seems pretty organized.

What does each row represent?
• It seems pretty obvious that each row represents a user giving a review of a business. The next thing we should do is to examine each row and label it by the type of data it contains. At this point, we can also use python to figure out just how big our dataset is. We can use the shape quality of a Dataframe to find this out, as shown:

30

yelp_raw_data.shape
(10000,10)

• It tells us that this dataset has 10000 rows and 10 columns. Another way to say this is that this dataset has 10,000 observations and 10 characteristics.

What does each column represent?
Note that we have 10 columns:
• **Business_id:** This is likely a unique identifier for the business the review is for. This would be at the nominal level because there is no natural order to this identifier.

• **Date:** This is probably the date at which the review was posted. Note that it seems to be only specific to the day, month, and year. Even though time is usually considered continuous, this column would likely be considered discrete and at the ordinal level because of the natural order that dates have.

• **Review_id:** This is likely a unique identifier for the review that each post represents. This would be at the nominal level because, again, there is no natural order to this identifier.

• **Stars:** From a quick look (don't worry; we will perform some further analysis soon), we can see that this is an ordered column that represents what the reviewer gave the restaurant as a final score. This is ordered and qualitative; so, this is at the ordinal level.

• **Text:** This is likely the raw text that each reviewer wrote. As with most text, we place this at the nominal level.

• **Type:** In the first five columns, all we see is the word review. This might be a column that identifies that each row is a review, implying that there might be another type of row other than a review. We will take a look at this later. We
place this at the nominal level.

31

• **User_id:** This is likely a unique identifier for the user who is writing the review. Just like the other unique IDs, we place this data at the nominal level.

Are there any missing data points?

• Perform an isnull operation. For example if your dataframe is called awesome_dataframe then try the python command awesome_dataframe. isnull().sum()which will show the number of missing values in each column.

Do we need to perform any transformations on the columns?

• At this point, we are looking for a few things. For example, will we need to change the scale of some of the quantitative data, or do we need to create dummy variables for the qualitative variables? As this dataset has only qualitative columns, we can only focus on transformations at the ordinal and nominal scale.

Before starting, let's go over some quick terminology for pandas, the python data exploration module.

Dataframes

When we read in a dataset, Pandas creates a custom object called Dataframe. Think of this as the python version of a spreadsheet (but way better). In this case, the variable, yelp_raw_data, is a Dataframe.

To check whether this is true in Python, type in the following code:

type(yelp_raw_data)
 # pandas.core.frame.DataFrame

Dataframes are two-dimensional in nature, meaning that they are organized in a row/column structure just as a spreadsheet is. The main benefits of using Dataframes over, say, a spreadsheet software would be that a Dataframe can handle much larger data than most common spreadsheet software. If you are familiar with the R language, you might recognize the word Dataframe. This is because the name was actually borrowed from the language!

As most of the data that we will deal with is organized, Dataframes are likely the most used object in pandas, second only to the Series object.

Series

The Series object is simply a Dataframe, but only with one dimension. Essentially, it is a list of data points. Each column of a Dataframe is considered to be a Series object. Let's check this. The first thing we need to do is grab a single column from our Dataframe; we generally use what is known as bracket notation. The following is an example:

yelp_raw_data['business_id'] # grabs a single column of the Dataframe

We will list the first few and last few rows:

0	*9yKzy9PApeiPPOUJEtnvkg*
1	*ZRJwVLyzEJq1VAihDhYiow*
2	*6oRAC4uyJCsJl1X0WZpVSA*
3	*_1QQZuf4zZOyFCvXc0o6Vg*
4	*6ozycU1RpktNG2-1BroVtw*
5	*-yxfBYGB6SEqszmxJxd97A*
6	*zp713qNhx8d9KCJJnrw1xA*

Let's use the type function to check that this column is a Series:

type(yelp_raw_data['business_id'])
 # pandas.core.series.Series

Exploration tips for qualitative data

Using these two Pandas objects, let's start performing some preliminary data exploration. For qualitative data, we will specifically look at the nominal and ordinal levels.

Nominal level columns

As we are at the nominal level, let's recall that at this level, data is qualitative and is described purely by name. In this dataset, this refers to the business_id, review_ id, text, type, and user_id. Let's use Pandas in order to dive a bit deeper, as shown here:

yelp_raw_data['business_id'].describe()

```
# count                    10000
# unique                   4174
# top                      JokKtdXU7zXHcr20Lrk29A
# freq                     37
```

The describe function will give us some quick stats about the column whose name we enter into the quotation marks. Note how Pandas automatically recognized that business_id was a qualitative column and gave us stats that make sense. When describe is called on a qualitative column, we will always get the following four items:

- *count:* How many values are filled in
- *unique:* How many unique values are filled in
- *top:* The name of the most common item in the dataset
- *freq:* How often the most common item appears in the dataset

At the nominal level, we are usually looking for a few things, that would signal a transformation:

- Do we have a reasonable number (usually under 20) of unique items?
- Is this column free text?
- Is this column completely unique across all rows?

So, for the business_id column, we have a count of 10000. Don't be fooled though! This does not mean that we have 10,000 businesses being reviewed here.

It just means that of the 10,000 rows of reviews, the business_id column is filled in all 10,000 times. The next qualifier, unique, tells us that we have 4174 unique businesses being reviewed in this dataset. The most reviewed business is business JokKtdXU7zXHcr20Lrk29A, which was reviewed 37 times.

yelp_raw_data['review_id'].describe()

# count	*10000*
# unique	*10000*
# top	*eTa5KD-LTgQv6UT1Zmijmw*
# freq	*1*

We have a count of 10000 and a unique of 10000. Think for a second, does this make sense? Think about what each row represents and what this column represents.

Of course it does! Each row of this dataset is supposed to represent a single, unique review of a business and this column is meant to serve as a unique identifier for a review; so, it makes sense that the review_id column has 10000 unique items in it.

So, why is eTa5KD-LTgQv6UT1Zmijmw the most common review? This is just a random choice from the 10,000 and means nothing.

yelp_raw_data['text'].describe()

count	*10000*
unique	*9998*
top	*This review is for the chain in general. The l...*
freq	*2*

This column, which represents the actual text people wrote, is interesting. We would imagine that this should also be similar to review_id in that there should be all unique text, because it would be weird if two people wrote exactly the same thing; but we have two reviews with the exact same text! Let's take a second to learn about Dataframe filtering to examine this further.

Filtering in Pandas

Let's talk a bit about how filtering works. Filtering rows based on certain criteria is quite easy in Pandas. In a Dataframe, if we wish to filter out rows based on some search criteria, we will need to go row by row and check whether or not a row satisfies that particular condition. Pandas handles this by passing in a Series of Trues and Falses (Booleans).

We literally pass into the Dataframe a list of True and False data that mean the following:

- *True:* This row satisfies the condition
- *False:* This row does not satisfy the condition

So, first let's make the conditions. In the following lines of code, I will grab the text that occurs twice:

duplicate_text = yelp_raw_data['text'].describe()['top']

Here is a snippet of the text:

"This review is for the chain in general. The location we went to is new so it isn't in Yelp yet. Once it is I will put this review there as well....... "

Right off the bat, we can guess that this might actually be one person who went to review two businesses that belong to the same chain and wrote the exact same review. However, this is just a guess right now.

36

Now that we have this text, let's use some magic to create that Series of true and false:

text_is_the_duplicate = yelp_raw_data['text'] == duplicate_text

Right away you might be confused. What we have done here is take the text column of the Dataframe and compared it to the string, duplicate_text. This is strange because we seem to be comparing a list of 10,000 elements to a single string. Of course, the answer should be a straight false, right?

The Pandas' Series has a very interesting feature in that if you compare the Series to an object, it will return another Series of Booleans of the same length where each true and false is the answer to the question, is this element the same as the element you are comparing it to? Very handy!

type(text_is_the_duplicate) # it is a Series of Trues and Falses

text_is_the_duplicate.head() # shows a few Falses out of the Series

In Python, we can add and subtract true and false as if they were 1 and 0, respectively. For example, True + False – True + False + True == 1. So, we can verify that this Series is correct by adding up all of the values. As only two of these rows should contain the duplicate text, the sum of the Series should only be 2, which it is!

This is shown as follows:
sum(text_is_the_duplicate) # == 2

Now that we have our Series of Booleans, we can pass it directly into our Dataframe, using bracket notation, and get our filtered rows, as illustrated:

filtered_dataframe = yelp_raw_data[text_is_the_duplicate]
 # the filtered Dataframe

filtered_dataframe

business id	date	review id	stars	text	type	user id	cool	useful	funny
4353	ywhaQ3Hc2XyxrrrvAA1JA	2012-06-16	wQ6pqmFFvkwERRgbuMu	2	This review is for the chain in general. The l...	review	HLatoZvadFi3ha99hv4JYzZMw	1	0	0
9658	nlmUaEEpfViz_ Mlfar-Aakm	2012-06-16	euAGER8Jbj1sJ8WezrpeRUA	2	This review is for the chain in general. The l...	review	HLatoZvadFi3ha99hv4JYzZMw	0	0	0

It seems that our suspicions were correct and one person, on the same day, gave the exact same review to two different business_id , presumably a part of the same chain. Let's keep moving along to the rest of our columns:

yelp_raw_data['type'].describe()

count	*10000*
unique	*1*
top	*review*
freq	*10000*

Remember this column? Turns out they are all the exact same type, namely review.

yelp_raw_data['user_id'].describe()

count	*10000*
unique	*6403*
top	*fczQCSmaWF78toLEmb0Zsw*
freq	*38*

Similar to the business_id column, all the 10000 values are filled in with 6403 unique users and one user reviewing 38 times! In this example, we won't have to perform any transformations.

Ordinal level columns

As far as ordinal columns go, we are looking at date and stars. For each of these columns, let's look at what the describe method brings back:

yelp_raw_data['stars'].describe()

```
# count               10000.000000
# mean                3.777500
# std                 1.214636
# min                 1.000000
# 25%                 3.000000
# 50%                 4.000000
# 75%                 5.000000
# max                 5.000000
```

Woah! Even though this column is ordinal, the describe method returned stats that we might expect for a quantitative column. This is because the software saw a bunch of numbers and just assumed that we wanted stats like the mean or the min and max. This is no problem. Let's use a method called value_counts to see the count distribution, as shown here:

yelp_raw_data['stars'].value_counts()

```
# 4                   3526
# 5                   3337
# 3                   1461
# 2                   927
# 1                   749
```

The value_counts method will return the distribution of values for any column. In this case, we see that the star rating 4 is the most common, with 3526 values, followed closely by the rating 5. We can also plot this data to get a nice visual. First, let's sort by star rating, and then use the prebuilt plot method to make a bar chart.

```
dates = yelp_raw_data['stars'].value_counts()
dates.sort()
dates.plot(kind='bar')
```

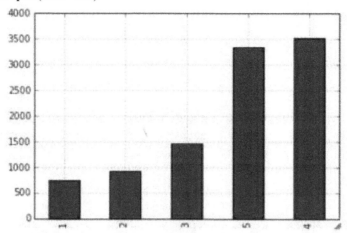

People are definitely more likely to give good star ratings over bad ones! We can follow this procedure for the date column. I will leave you to try it on your own. For now, let's look at a new dataset.

Dataset 2 – titanic

The titanic dataset contains a sample of people who were on the Titanic when it struck an iceberg in 1912. Let's go ahead and import it, as shown here:

titanic = pd.read_csv('short_titanic.csv')
titanic.head()

	Survived	Pclass	Name	Sex	Age
0	0	3	Braund, Mr. Owen Harris	male	22
1	1	1	Cumings, Mrs. John Bradley (Florence Briggs Th...	female	38
2	1	3	Heikkinen, Miss. Laina	female	26
3	1	1	Futrelle, Mrs. Jacques Heath (Lily May Peel)	female	35
4	0	3	Allen, Mr. William Henry	male	35

This Dataframe usually has more columns; however, for our example, we will only focus on the given columns.

This data is definitely organized in a row/column structure, as is most spreadsheet data. Let's take a quick peek as to its size, as shown here:

titanic.shape
 # (891, 5)

So, we have 891 rows and 5 columns. Each row seems to represent a single passenger on the ship and as far as columns are concerned, the following list tells us what they indicate:

- Survived: This is a binary variable that indicates whether or not the passenger survived the accident (1 if they survived, 0 if they died). This would likely be at the nominal level because there are only two options.
- Pclass: This is the class that the passenger was traveling in (3 for third class, and so on). This is at the ordinal level.
- Name: This is the name of the passenger, and it is definitely at the nominal level.

- Sex: This indicates the gender of the passenger. It is at the nominal level.
- Age: This one is a bit tricky. Arguably, you may place age at either a qualitative or quantitative level, however, I think that age belongs to a quantitative state, and thus, to the ratio level.

As far as transformations are concerned, usually, we want all columns to be numerical, regardless of their qualitative state. This means that Name and Sex will have to be converted into numerical columns somehow. For Sex, we can change the column to hold 1 if the passenger was female and 0 if they were male. Let's use Pandas to make the change. We will have to import another Python module, called

41

numpy or numerical Python, as illustrated:
import numpy as np titanic['Sex'] = np.where(titanic['Sex']=='female',
1, 0)

The np.where method takes in three things:

- A list of Booleans (true or false)
- A new value
- A backup value

The method will replace all true with the first value (in this case 1) and the false with the second value (in this case 0), leaving us with a new numerical column that represents the same thing as the original Sex column.

titanic['Sex']

# 0	0
# 1	1
# 2	1
# 3	1
# 4	0
# 5	0
# 6	0
# 7	0

Let's use a shortcut and describe all the columns at once, as shown:

titanic.describe()

	Survived	Pclass	Sex	Age
count	891.000000	891.000000	891.000000	714.000000
mean	0.383838	2.308642	0.352413	29.699118
std	0.486592	0.836071	0.477990	14.526497
min	0.000000	1.000000	0.000000	0.420000
25%	0.000000	2.000000	0.000000	20.125000
50%	0.000000	3.000000	0.000000	28.000000
75%	1.000000	3.000000	1.000000	38.000000
max	1.000000	3.000000	1.000000	80.000000

Note how our qualitative columns are being treated as quantitative; however, I'm looking for something irrelevant to the data type. Note the count row: Survived, Pclass, and Sex all have 891 values (the number of rows), but Age only has 714 values. Some are missing! To double verify, let's use the Pandas functions, called isnull and sum, as shown:

titanic.isnull().sum()

Survived   0
Pclass   0
Name   0
Sex   0
Age   177

This will show us the number of missing values in each column. So, Age is the only column with missing values to deal with.

When dealing with missing values, you usually have the following two options:

- Drop the row with the missing value
- Try to fill it in

Dropping the row is the easy choice; however, you run the risk of losing valuable data! For example, in this case, we have 177 missing age values (891-714) which is nearly 20% of the data. To fill in the data, we could either go back to the history books, find each person one by one, and fill in their age, or we can fill in the age with a placeholder value.

Let's fill in each missing value of the Age column with the overall average age of the people in the dataset. For this, we will use two new methods, called mean and fillna. We use isnull to tell us which values are null and the mean function to give us the average value of the Age column. fillna is a Pandas method that replaces null values with a given value.

print sum(titanic['Age'].isnull()) # == 177 missing values

average_age = titanic['Age'].mean() # get the average age

titanic['Age'].fillna(average_age, inplace = True) #use the fillna method to remove null values

print sum(titanic['Age'].isnull()) # == 0 missing values

We're done! We have replaced each value with 26.69, the average age in the dataset.

titanic.isnull().sum()

Survived	*0*
Pclass	*0*
Name	*0*
Sex	*0*
Age	*0*

Great! Nothing is missing, and we did not have to remove any rows.

titanic.head()

	Survived	Pclass	Name	Sex	Age
0	0	3	Braund, Mr. Owen Harris	0	22
1	1	1	Cumings, Mrs. John Bradley (Florence Briggs Th...	1	38
2	1	3	Heikkinen, Miss. Laina	1	26
3	1	1	Futrelle, Mrs. Jacques Heath (Lily May Peel)	1	35
4	0	3	Allen, Mr. William Henry	0	35

At this point, we could start getting a bit more complicated with our questions. For example, what is the average age for a female or a male? To answer this, we can filter by each gender and take the mean age. Pandas has a built-in function for this, called groupby, as illustrated here:

titanic.groupby('Sex')['Age'].mean()

This means group the data by the Sex column, and then give me the mean of age for each group. This gives us the following output:

Sex

0   30.505824
1   28.216730

We will ask more of these difficult and complex questions and will be able to answer them with Python and statistics.

Chapter IV
Fundamentals of Mathematics

It's time to start looking at some basic mathematic principles that are handy when dealing with data science. The word math tends to strike fear in the hearts of many, but I aim to make this as enjoyable as possible. In this chapter, we will go over the basics of the following topics:

* Basic symbols/terminology
* Logarithms/exponents
* The set theory
* Calculus
* Matrix (linear) algebra

We will also cover other fields of mathematics. Moreover, we will see how to apply each of these to various aspects of data science as well as other scientific endeavors.

Recall that, in a previous chapter, we identified math as being one of the three key components of data science. In this chapter, I will introduce concepts that will become important later on in this book—when looking at probabilistic and statistical models—and I will also be looking at concepts that will be useful in this chapter. Regardless of this, all of the concepts in this chapter should be considered fundamentals in your quest to become a data scientist.

4.1 Mathematics as a discipline

Mathematics, as a science, is one of the oldest known forms of logical thinking by mankind. Since ancient Mesopotamia and likely before (3,000 BCE), humans have been relying on arithmetic and more challenging forms of math to answer life's biggest questions. Today, we rely on math for most aspects of our daily life; yes, I know that sounds cliché, but I mean it. Whether you are watering your plants or feeding your dog, your internal mathematical engine is constantly spinning—calculating how much water the plant had per day over the last week and predicting the next time your dog will be hungry given that they eat right now. Whether or not you are consciously using the principles of math, the concepts live deep inside everyone's brains. It's my job as a math teacher to get you to realize it.

4.2 Basic symbols and terminology

First, let's take a look at the most basic symbols that are used in the mathematical process as well as some more subtle notations used by data scientists.

Vectors and matrices

A vector is defined as an object with both magnitude and direction. This definition, however, is a bit complicated for our use. For our purpose, a vector is simply a 1-dimensional array representing a series of numbers. Put in another way, a vector is a list of numbers.

It is generally represented using an arrow or bold font, as shown:

$$\vec{x} \quad or \quad x$$

Vectors are broken into components, which are individual members of the vector. We use index notations to denote the element that we are referring to, as illustrated:

$$\text{If} \quad \vec{x} = \begin{pmatrix} 3 \\ 6 \\ 8 \end{pmatrix} \quad \text{then} \quad x_1 = 3$$

In math, we generally refer to the first element as index 1, as opposed to computer science, where we generally refer to the first element as index 0. It is important to remember what index system you are using.

In Python, we can represent arrays in many ways. We could simply use a Python list to represent the preceding array:

$$x = [3, \ 6, \ 8]$$

47

However, it is better to use the numpy array type to represent arrays, as shown, because it gives us much more utility when performing vector operations:

import numpy as np
x = np.array([3, 6, 8])

Regardless of the Python representation, vectors give us a simple way of storing multiple dimensions of a single data point/observation.

Consider that we measure the average satisfaction rating (0-100) of employees for three departments of a company as being 57 for HR, 89 for engineering, and 94 for management. We can represent this as a vector with the following formula:

$$x = \begin{pmatrix} x_1 \\ x_2 \\ x_3 \end{pmatrix} = \begin{pmatrix} 57 \\ 89 \\ 94 \end{pmatrix}$$

This vector holds three different bits of information about our data. This is the perfect use of a vector in data science.
You can also think of a vector as being the theoretical generalization of Panda's Series object. So, naturally, we need something to represent the Dataframe. We can extend our notion of an array to move beyond a single dimension and represent data in multiple dimensions.

A matrix is a 2-dimensional representation of arrays of numbers. Matrices (plural) have two main characteristics that we need to be aware of. The dimension of thematrix, denoted as n x m (n by m), tells us that the matrix has n rows and m columns.
Matrices are generally denoted using a capital, bold-faced letter, such as X. Consider the following example:

$$\begin{pmatrix} 3 & 4 \\ 8 & 55 \\ 5 & 9 \end{pmatrix}$$

This is a 3 x 2 (3 by 2) matrix because it has three rows and two columns.

The matrix is our generalization of the Pandas Dataframe. It is arguably one of the most important mathematical objects in our toolkit. It is used to hold organized information, in our case, data.

Revisiting our previous example, let's say we have three offices in different locations, each with the same three departments: HR, engineering, and management. We could make three different vectors, each holding a different office's satisfaction scores, as shown:

$$x = \begin{pmatrix} 57 \\ 89 \\ 94 \end{pmatrix}, y = \begin{pmatrix} 67 \\ 87 \\ 84 \end{pmatrix}, z = \begin{pmatrix} 65 \\ 98 \\ 60 \end{pmatrix}$$

However, this is not only cumbersome, but also unscalable. What if you have 100 different offices? Then we would need to have 100 different 1-dimensional arrays to hold this information.

This is where a matrix alleviates this problem. Let's make a matrix where each row represents a different department and each column represents a different office, as shown:

	Office 1	Office 2	Office 3
HR	57	67	65
Engineering	89	87	98
Management	94	84	60

This is much more natural. Now, let's strip away the labels, and we are left with a matrix!

$$X = \begin{pmatrix} 57 & 67 & 65 \\ 89 & 87 & 98 \\ 94 & 84 & 60 \end{pmatrix}$$

Arithmetic symbols

In this section, we will go over some symbols associated with basic arithmetic that appear in most, if not all, data science tutorials and books.

Summation

The uppercase sigma symbol is a universal symbol for addition. Whatever is to the right of the sigma symbol is usually something iterable, meaning that we can go over it one by one (for example, a vector).

For example, let's create the representation of a vector:

$$X = [1, 2, 3, 4, 5]$$

To find the sum of the content, we can use the following formula:

$$\sum x_i = 15$$

In Python, we can use the following formula:

$$sum(x) \ \# == 15$$

For example, the formula for calculating the mean of a series of numbers is quite common. If we have a vector (x) of length n, the mean of the vector can be calculated as follows:

$$mean = \frac{1}{n} \sum x_i$$

This means that we will add up each element of x, denoted by x_i, and then multiply the sum by 1/n, otherwise known as dividing by n, the length of the vector.

Proportional

The lowercase alpha symbol represents values that are proportional to each other. This means that as one value changes, so does the other. The direction in which the values move depends on how the values are proportional. Values can either vary directly or indirectly. If values vary directly, they both move in the same direction (as one goes up, so does the other). If they vary indirectly, they move in opposite directions (if one goes down, the other goes up).

Consider the following examples:

• The sales of a company vary directly with the number of customers. This can be written as .
• Gas prices vary (usually) indirectly with oil availability, meaning that as the availability of oil goes down (it's more scarce), gas prices will go up. This can be denoted as .

Later on, we will see a very important formula called the Bayes formula, which includes a variation symbol.

Dot product

The dot product is an operator like addition and multiplication. It is used to combine two vectors, as shown:

$$\begin{pmatrix} 3 \\ 7 \end{pmatrix} \cdot \begin{pmatrix} 9 \\ 5 \end{pmatrix} = 3 * 9 + 7 * 5 = 62$$

So, what does this mean? Let's say we have a vector that represents a customer's sentiments towards three genres of movies—comedy, romantic, and action.

Consider that, on a scale of 1-5, a customer loves comedies, hates romantic movies, and is alright with action movies. We might represent this as follows:

$$\begin{pmatrix} 5 \\ 1 \\ 3 \end{pmatrix}$$

Here:
• 5 denotes the love for comedies,
• 1 is the hatred for romantic
• 3 is the indifference of action

Now, let's assume that we have two new movies, one of which is a romantic comedy and the other is a funny action movie. The movies would have their own vector of qualities, as shown:

$$m_1 = \begin{pmatrix} 4 \\ 5 \\ 1 \end{pmatrix} \text{ and } m_2 = \begin{pmatrix} 5 \\ 1 \\ 5 \end{pmatrix}$$

Here, is our romantic comedy and is our funny action movie.
In order to make a recommendation, we will apply the dot product between the customer's preferences for each movie. The higher value will win and, therefore, will be recommended to the user.

Let's compute the recommendation score for each movie. For movie 1, we want to compute:

$$\begin{pmatrix} 5 \\ 1 \\ 3 \end{pmatrix} \cdot \begin{pmatrix} 4 \\ 5 \\ 1 \end{pmatrix}$$

We can think of this problem as such:

Customer: M_2

$$\begin{pmatrix} 5 \\ 1 \\ 3 \end{pmatrix} \cdot \begin{pmatrix} 4 \\ 5 \\ 1 \end{pmatrix}$$

$(5.4) \longrightarrow$ user loves comedies and this move is funny
$+$
$= (1.5) \longrightarrow$ user hates romance but this move is romantic
$+$
$(3.1) \longrightarrow$ user doesn't mind action and the move is not action packed
_____
28

The answer we obtain is 28, but what does this number mean? On what scale is it? Well, the best score anyone can ever get is when all values are 5, making the outcome as follows:

$$\begin{pmatrix} 5 \\ 5 \\ 5 \end{pmatrix} \cdot \begin{pmatrix} 5 \\ 5 \\ 5 \end{pmatrix} = 5^2 + 5^2 + 5^2 = 75$$

The lowest possible score is when all values are 1, as shown:

$$\begin{pmatrix} 1 \\ 1 \\ 1 \end{pmatrix} \cdot \begin{pmatrix} 1 \\ 1 \\ 1 \end{pmatrix} = 1^2 + 1^2 + 1^2 = 3$$

So, we must think about 28 on a scale from 3-75. To do this, imagine a number line from 3 to 75 and where 28 would be on it. This is illustrated as follows:

```
 |---------+----------------|
 3       28                75
```

Not that far. Let's try for movie 2:

$$\begin{pmatrix} 5 \\ 1 \\ 3 \end{pmatrix} \cdot \begin{pmatrix} 5 \\ 1 \\ 5 \end{pmatrix} = (5*5) + (1*1) + (3*5) = 41$$

Graphs

No doubt you have encountered dozens, if not hundreds, of graphs in your life so far. I'd like to mostly talk about conventions with regard to graphs and notations.

y | ___ x

This is a basic Cartesian graph (x and y coordinate). The x and y notation are very standard but sometimes do not entirely explain the big picture. We sometimes refer to the x variable as being the independent variable and the y as the dependent variable. This is because when we write functions, we tend to speak about them as being y is a function of x, meaning that the value of y is dependent on the value of x. This is what a graph is trying to show.

y | (x_2, y_2) (x_1, y_1) ___ x

Suppose we have two points on a graph, as shown:

Logarithms/exponents

An exponent tells you how many times you have to multiply a number to itself, as illustrated:

$$2^4 = 2 \cdot 2 \cdot 2 \cdot 2 = 16$$

A logarithm is the number that answers the question: "what exponent gets me from the base to this other number?" This can be denoted as follows:

$$\log_2(16) = 4$$

base   logarithm

If these two concepts seem similar, then you are correct! Exponents and logarithms are heavily related. In fact, the words exponent and logarithm actually mean the same thing! A logarithm is an exponent. The preceding two equations are actually two versions of the same thing. The basic idea is that 2 times 2 times 2 times 2 is 16.

The following is a depiction of how we can use both versions to say the same thing. Note how I use arrows to move from the log formula to the exponent formula:

$$\log_2(16) = 4 \leftrightarrow 2^4 = 16$$

Consider the following examples:

- $\log_3 81 = 4$ because $3^4 = 81$
- $\log_5 125 = 3$ because $5^3 = 125$

Note something interesting, if we rewrite the first equation to be:

$$\log_3 81 = 4$$

We then replace 81 with the equivalent statement, 34, as follows:

$$\log_3 3^4 = 4$$

We can note something interesting: the 3s seem to cancel out. This is actually very important when dealing with numbers more difficult to work with than 3s and 4s. Exponents and logarithms are most important when dealing with growth. More often than not, if some quantity is growing (or declining in growth), an exponent/ logarithm can help model this behavior.

For example, the number e is around 2.718 and has many practical applications. A very common application is growth calculation for money. Suppose you have $5,000 deposited in a bank with continuously compounded interest at the rate of 3%, then we can use the following formula to model the growth of our deposit:

$$A = Pe^{rt}$$

Where:
- A denotes the final amount
- P denotes the principal investment (5000)
- e denotes constant (2.718)
- r denotes the rate of growth (.03)
- t denotes the time (in years)
-

We are curious, when will our investment double? How long would I have to have my money in this investment to achieve 100% growth? Basically:

$$10000 = 5000e^{.03t}$$

Is the formula we wish to solve:

$$10000 = 5000e^{.03t}$$
$$2 = e^{.03t} \quad (divide\ by\ 5000\ on\ both\ sides)$$

At this point, we have a variable in the exponent that we want to solve. When this happens, we can use the logarithm notation to figure it out!

$$2 = e^{.03t} \leftrightarrow \log_e(2) = .03t$$

56

4.3 Linear algebra

Remember the movie recommendation engine we looked at earlier? What if we had 10,000 movies to recommend and we had to choose only 10 to give to the user? We'd have to take a dot product between the user profile and each of the 10,000 movies.

Linear algebra provides the tools to make these calculations much more efficient. It is an area of mathematics that deals with the math of matrices and vectors. It has the aim of breaking down these objects and reconstructing them in order to provide practical applications. Let's look at a few linear algebra rules before proceeding.

Matrix multiplication

Like numbers, we can multiple matrices together. Multiplying matrices is, in essence, a mass produced way of taking several dot products at once. Let's, for example, try to multiple the following matrices:

$$\begin{pmatrix} 1 & 5 \\ 5 & 8 \\ 7 & 8 \end{pmatrix} \cdot \begin{pmatrix} 3 & 4 \\ 2 & 5 \end{pmatrix}$$

A couple of things:

- Unlike numbers, multiplication is not commutative, meaning that the order in which you multiply matrices matters a great deal.
- In order to multiply matrices, their dimensions must match up. This means that the first matrix must have the same number of columns as the second matrix has rows.

To remember this, write out the dimensions of the matrices. In this case, we have a 3 x 2 times a 2 x 2 matrix. You can multiple matrices together if the second number in the first dimension pair is the same as the first number in the second dimension pair.

$$3 \times \boxed{2 \cdot 2} \times 2$$

The resulting matrix will always have dimensions equal to the outer numbers in the dimension pairs (the ones you did not circle in the second point). In this case, the resulting matrix will have a dimension of 3 x 2.

How to multiply matrices

To multiply matrices, there is actually a quite simple procedure. Essentially, we are performing a bunch of dot products.

$$\begin{pmatrix} 1 & 5 \\ 5 & 8 \\ 7 & 8 \end{pmatrix} \cdot \begin{pmatrix} 3 & 4 \\ 2 & 5 \end{pmatrix}$$

Recall our earlier sample problem, which was as follows: We know that our resulting matrix will have a dimension of 3 x 2. So, we know it will look something like the following:

$$\begin{pmatrix} m_{11} & m_{12} \\ m_{21} & m_{22} \\ m_{31} & m_{32} \end{pmatrix}$$

The element is the result of the dot product of the xth row of the first matrix and the yth column of the second matrix. Let's solve a few:

$$m_{11} = \begin{pmatrix} 1 \\ 5 \end{pmatrix} \cdot \begin{pmatrix} 3 \\ 2 \end{pmatrix} = 13$$

$$m_{12} = \begin{pmatrix} 1 \\ 5 \end{pmatrix} \cdot \begin{pmatrix} 4 \\ 5 \end{pmatrix} = 29$$

Moving on, we will eventually get a resulting matrix as follows:

$$\begin{pmatrix} 13 & 29 \\ 31 & 60 \\ 37 & 68 \end{pmatrix}$$

Way to go! Let's come back to the movie recommendation example. Recall the user's movie genre preferences of comedy, romance, and action, which are illustrated as follows:

$$U = user\ prefs = \begin{pmatrix} 5 \\ 1 \\ 3 \end{pmatrix}$$

Now suppose we have 10,000 movies, all with a rating for these three categories. To make a recommendation, we need to take the dot product of the preference vector with each of the 10,000 movies. We can use matrix multiplication to represent this.

Instead of writing them all out, let's express it using the matrix notation. We already have U, defined here as the user's preference vector (it can also be thought of as a 3 x 1 matrix), and we also need a movie matrix: So, now we have two matrices, one is *3 x 1* and the other is *3 x 10,000*. We can't

multiply these matrices as they are because the dimensions do not work out. We will have to change *U* a bit. We can take the *transpose* of the matrix (turning all rows into columns and columns into rows). This will switch the dimensions around:

$$U^T = transpose\ of\ U = (513)$$

So, now we have two matrices that can be multiplied together. To visualize what this looks like:

$$
(5\ 1\ 3\ 5\ 1\ 3) \cdot \begin{pmatrix} 452 \\ \cdots \\ 151 \end{pmatrix}
$$

1×3   3×10000

The resulting matrix will be a 1 x 1,000 matrix (a vector) of 10,000 predictions for each individual movie. Let's try this out in Python!

```
import numpy as np

# create user preferences
user_pref = np.array([5, 1, 3])

# create a random movie matrix of 10,000 movies
movies = np.random.randint(5,size=(3,1000))+1

# Note that the randint will make random integers from 0-4
# so I added a 1 at the end to increase the scale from 1-5
```

We are using the numpy array function to create our matrices. We will have both a user_pref and a movies matrix to represent our data.

To check our dimensions, we can use the numpy shape variable, as shown:

```
print user_pref.shape # (1, 3)
print movies.shape # (3, 1000)
```

This checks out. Last but not least, let's use the matrix multiplication method of numpy (called dot) to perform the operation, as illustrated:

 # np.dot does both dot products and matrix multiplication
np.dot(user_pref, movies)

The result is an array of integers that represents the recommendations of each movie.

For a quick extension of this, let's run some code that predicts across more than
10,000 movies, as shown:

import time

for num_movies in (10000, 100000, 1000000, 10000000, 100000000):

movies = np.random.randint(5,size=(3, movies))+1
now = time.time()
np.dot(user_pref, movies)
print (time.time() - now), "seconds to run", movies, "movies"

0.000160932540894 seconds to run 10000 movies
0.00121188163757 seconds to run 100000 movies
0.0105860233307 seconds to run 1000000 movies
0.096577167511 seconds to run 10000000 movies
4.16197991371 seconds to run 100000000 movies

It took only a bit over 4 seconds to run through 100,000,000 movies using matrix multiplication.

Chapter V
Machine Learning Essentials

Machine learning has become quite the phrase of the decade. It seems as though every time we hear about the next greatest startup or turn on the news, we hear something about a revolutionary piece of machine learning technology and how it will change the way we live.

This chapter focuses on machine learning as a practical part of data science. We will cover the following topics in this chapter:

•   Defining the different types of machine learning, along with examples of each kind
•   Areas in regression, classification, and more
•   What is machine learning and how it is used in data science
•   The differences between machine learning and statistical modeling and how machine learning is a broader category of the latter

Our aim will be to utilize statistics, probability, and algorithmic thinking in order to understand and apply essential machine learning skills to practical industries, such as marketing. Examples will include predicting star ratings of restaurant reviews, predicting the presence of a disease, spam e-mail detection, and much more. This chapter focuses more on machine learning as a whole and a single statistical model. The subsequent chapters will deal with many more models, some of which are much more complex.

We will also turn our focus on metrics, which tell us how effective our models are. We will use metrics in order to conclude results and make predictions using machine learning.

5.1 What is machine learning

It wouldn't make sense to continue without a concrete definition of what machine learning is. Well, let's back up for a minute. In Chapter 1, How to Sound Like a Data Scientist, we defined machine learning as giving computers the ability to learn from data without being given explicit rules by a programmer. This definition still holds true. Machine learning is concerned with the ability to ascertain certain patterns (signals) out of data, even if the data has inherent errors in it (noise).

Machine learning models are able to learn from data without the explicit help of a human. That is the main difference between machine learning models and classical algorithms. Classical algorithms are told how to find the best answer in a complex system and the algorithm then searches for these best solutions and often works faster and more efficiently than a human. However, the bottleneck here is that the human has to first come up with the best solution. In machine learning, the model is not told the best solution and instead, is given several examples of the problem and is told, figure out the best solution.

Machine learning is just another tool in the tool belt of a data scientist. It is on the same level as statistical tests (chi-square or t-tests) or uses base probability/statistics to estimate population parameters. Machine learning is often regarded as the only thing data scientists know how to do, and this is simply untrue. A true data scientist is able to recognize when machine learning is applicable and more importantly, when it is not.

Machine learning is a game of correlations and relationships. Most machine learning algorithms in existence are concerned with finding and/or exploiting relationships between datasets (often represented as columns in a Pandas Dataframe). Once machine learning algorithms can pinpoint on certain correlations, the model can either use these relationships to predict future observations or generalize the data to reveal interesting patterns.

Perhaps a great way to explain machine learning is to offer an example of a problem coupled with two possible solutions: one using a machine learning algorithm and the other utilizing a non-machine learning algorithm.

Example – facial recognition

This problem is very well documented. Given a picture of a face, whose face does it belong to? However, I argue that there is a more important question that must be asked even before this. Suppose you wish to implement a home security system that recognizes who is entering your house. Most likely, during the day, your house will be empty most of the time and the facial recognition must kick in only if there is a person in the shot. This is exactly the question I propose we try and solve—given a photo, is there a face in it?

Given this problem, I propose the following two solutions:

- The non-machine learning algorithm that will define a face as having a roundish structure, two eyes, hair, nose, and so on. The algorithm then looks for these hard-coded features in the photo and returns whether or not it was able to find any of these features.
- The machine learning algorithm will work a bit differently. The model will only be given several pictures of faces and non-faces that are labeled as such. From the examples (called training sets) it would figure out its own definition of a face.

The machine learning version of the solution is never told what a face is, it is merely given several examples, some with faces, and some without. It is then up to the machine learning model to figure out the difference between the two. Once it figures out the difference between the two, it uses this information to take in a picture and predict whether or not there is a face in the new picture. For example, to train the model, we will give it the following three images:

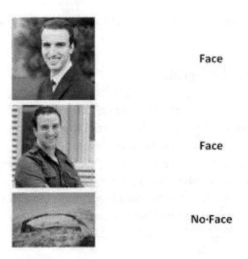

Face

Face

No·Face

The model will then figure out the difference between the pictures labeled as Face and the images labeled as No Face and be able to use that difference to find faces in the future photos.

5.2 Machine learning isn't perfect

There are many caveats of machine learning. Many are specific to different models being implemented, but there are some assumptions that are universal for any machine learning model, as follows:

- The data used is, for the most part, is preprocessed and cleaned using the methods outlined in the earlier chapters.

  Almost no machine learning model will tolerate dirty data with missing values or categorical values. Use dummy variables and filling/dropping techniques to handle these discrepancies.

- Each row of a cleaned dataset represents a single observation of the environment we are trying to model.

- If our goal is to find relationships between variables, then there is an assumption that there is some kind of relationship between these variables.

  This assumption is particularly important. Many machine learning models take this assumption very seriously. These models are not able to communicate that there might not be a relationship.

- Machine learning models are generally considered semiautomatic, which means that intelligent decisions by humans are still needed. The machine is very smart but has a hard time putting things into context.

  The output of most models is a series of numbers and metrics attempting to quantify how well the model did. It is up to a human to put these metrics into perspective and communicate the results to an audience

- Most machine learning models are sensitive to noisy data.

  This means that the models get confused when you include data that doesn't make sense. For example, if you are attempting to find relationships between economic data around the world and one of your columns is puppy adoption rates in the capital city, that information is likely not to be relevant and will confuse the model.

These assumptions will come up again and again when dealing with machine learning. They are all too important and often ignored by novice data scientists.

5.3 How does machine learning work

Each flavor of machine learning and each individual model works in very different ways, exploiting different parts of mathematics and data science. However, in general, machine learning works by taking in data, finding relationships within the data, and giving as output what the model learned, as illustrated in the following diagram:

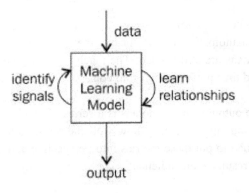

An overview of machine learning models

As we explore the different types of machine learning models, we will see how they manipulate data differently and come up with different outputs for different applications.

5.4 Types of machine learning

There are many ways to segment machine learning and dive deeper. In Chapter 1, How to Sound Like a Data Scientist, I mentioned statistical and probabilistic models. These models utilize statistics and probability, which we've seen in the previous chapters, in order to find relationships between data and make predictions. In this chapter, we will implement both types of models. In the following chapter, we will see machine learning outside the rigid mathematical world of statistics/probability. One can segment machine learning models by different characteristics, including:

- The types of data/organic structures they utilize (tree/graph/neural network)

- The field of mathematics they are most related to (statistical/probabilistic)
- The level of computation required to train (deep learning)

For the purpose of education, I will offer my own breakdown of machine learning models. Branching off of the top level of machine learning, there are the following three subsets:

- Supervised learning
- Unsupervised learning
- Reinforcement learning

Supervised learning

Simply put, supervised learning finds associations between features of a dataset and a target variable. For example, supervised learning models might try to find the association between a person's health features (heart rate, obesity level, and so on) and that person's risk of having a heart attack (the target variable).

These associations allow supervised models to make predictions based on past examples. This is often the first thing that comes to people's minds when they hear the phrase, machine learning, but it in no way does it encompass the realm of machine learning. Supervised machine learning models are often called predictive analytics models, named for their ability to predict the future based on the past.

Supervised machine learning requires a certain type of data called labeled data. This means that we must teach our model by giving it historical examples that are labeled with the correct answer. Recall the facial recognition example. That is a supervised learning model because we are training our model with the previous pictures labeled as either face or not face, and then asking the model to predict whether or not a new picture has a face in it.

Specifically, supervised learning works using parts of the data to predict another part. First, we must separate data into two parts, as follows:

- The predictors, which are the columns that will be used to make our prediction.
- These are sometimes called features, inputs, variables, and independent variables.
- The response, which is the column that we wish to predict.
- This is sometimes called outcome, label, target, and dependent variable.

Supervised learning attempts to find a relationship between the predictors and the response in order to make a prediction. The idea is that in the future a data observation will present itself and we will only know the predictors. The model will then have to use the predictors to make an accurate prediction of the response value.

Example – heart attack prediction

Suppose we wish to predict if someone will have a heart attack within a year. To predict this, we are given that person's cholesterol, blood pressure, height, their smoking habits, and perhaps more. From this data, we must ascertain the likelihood of a heart attack. Suppose, to make this prediction, we look at the previous patients and their medical history. As these are previous patients, we know not only their predictors (cholesterol, blood pressure, and so on), but we also know if they actually had a heart attack (because it already happened!).

This is a supervised machine learning problem because we are:
- Making a prediction about someone
- Using historical training data to find relationships between medical variables and heart attacks

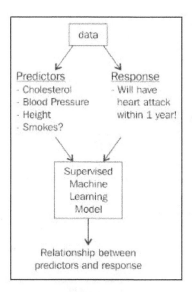

The hope here is that a patient will walk in tomorrow and our model will be able to identify whether or not the patient is at risk for a heart attack based on her/his conditions (just like a doctor would!).

As the model sees more and more labeled data, it adjusts itself in order to match the correct labels given to us. We can use different metrics (explained later in this chapter) to pinpoint exactly how well our supervised machine learning model is doing and how it can better adjust itself.

One of the biggest drawbacks of supervised machine learning is that we need this labeled data, which can be very difficult to get a hold of. Suppose we wish to predict heart attacks, we might need thousands of patients along with all of their filled in medical information and years' worth of follow-up records for each person, which could be a nightmare to obtain.

In short, supervised models use historical labeled data in order to make predictions about the future. Some possible applications for supervised learning include:

• Stock price predictions
• Weather predictions
• Crime predictions

Note how each of the preceding examples uses the word prediction, which makes sense seeing how I emphasized supervised learning's ability to make predictions about the future. Predictions, however, are not where the story ends.

Here is a visualization of how supervised models use labeled data to fit themselves and prepare themselves to make predictions:

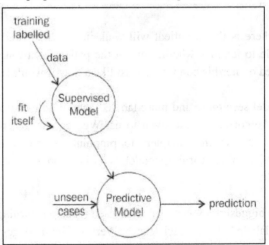

Note how the supervised model learns from a bunch of training data and then, when it is ready, it looks at unseen cases and outputs a prediction.

It's not only about predictions

Supervised learning exploits the relationship between the predictors and the response to make predictions, but sometimes, it is enough just knowing that there even is a relationship. Suppose we are using a supervised machine learning model to predict whether or not a customer will purchase a given item. A possible dataset might look as follows:

Person ID	Age	Gender	Employed?	Bought the product?
1	63	F	N	Y
2	24	M	Y	N

Note that, in this case, our predictors are Age, Gender, and Employed, while our response is Bought the product? This is because we want to see if, given someone's age, gender, and employment status, they will buy the product.

Assume that a model is trained on this data and can make accurate predictions about whether or not someone will buy something. That, in and of itself, is exciting but there's something else that is arguably even more exciting. The fact that we could make accurate predictions implies that there is a relationship between these variables, which means that to know if someone will buy your product, you only need to know their age, gender, and employment status! This might contradict the previous market research indicating that much more must be known about a potential customer to make such a prediction.

This speaks to supervised machine learning's ability to understand which predictors affect the response and how. For example, are women more likely to buy the product, which age groups are prone to decline the product, is there a combination of age and gender that is a better predictor than any one column on its own? As someone's age increases, do their chances of buying the product go up, down, or stay the same?
It is also possible that all the columns are not necessary. A possible output of a machine learning might suggest that only certain columns are necessary to make the prediction and that the other columns are

only noise (they do not correlate to the response and therefore confuse the model).

Types of supervised learning

There are, in general, two types of supervised learning models: regression and classification. The difference between the two is quite simple and lies in the response variable.

Regression

Regression models attempt to predict a continuous response. This means that the response can take on a range of infinite values. Consider the following examples:

• Dollar amounts
    ∘∘ Salary
    ∘∘ Budget
• Temperature
• Time
    ∘∘ Generally recorded in seconds or minutes

Classification

Classification attempts to predict a categorical response, which means that the response only has a finite amount of choices. Examples include the ones given as follows:

• Cancer grade (1, 2, 3, 4, 5)
• True/False questions, such as the following examples:
    ∘∘ "Will this person have a heart attack within a year?"
    ∘∘ "Will you get this job?"
• Given a photo of a face, who does this face belong to? (facial recognition)
• Predict the year someone was born:
    ∘∘ Note that there are many possible answers (over 100) but still finitely many more

Example – regression

The following graphs show a relationship between three categorical variables (age, year they were born, and education level) and a person's wage:

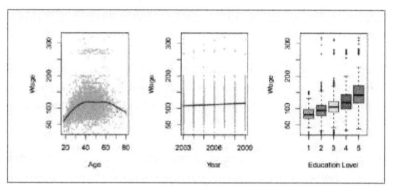

Source:
https://lagunita.stanford.edu/c4x/HumanitiesScience/StatLearning/asset/introduction.pdf

Note that even though each predictor is categorical, this example is regressive because the y axis, our dependent variable, our response, is continuous.

Our earlier heart attack example is classification because the response was will this person have a heart attack within a year?, which has only two possible answers:
Yes or No.

Data is in the eyes of the beholder

Sometimes, it can be tricky to decide whether or not you should use classification or regression. Consider that we are interested in the weather outside. We could ask the question, how hot is it outside?, in which case your answer is on a continuous scale, and some possible answers are 60.7 degrees, or 98 degrees. However, as an exercise, go and ask 10 people what the temperature is outside. I guarantee you that someone (if not most people) will not answer in some exact degrees but will bucket their answer and say something like it's in the 60s.

We might wish to consider this problem as a classification problem, where the response variable is no longer in exact degrees but is in a bucket. There would only be a finite number of buckets in theory, making the model perhaps learn the differences between 60s and 70s a bit better.

Unsupervised learning

The second type of machine learning does not deal with predictions but has a much more open objective. Unsupervised learning takes in a set of predictors and utilizes relationships between the predictors in order to accomplish tasks, such as the following:

- Reducing the dimension of the data by condensing variables together.
- An example of this would be file compression. Compression works by utilizing patterns in the data and representing the data in a smaller format.

- Finding groups of observations that behave similarly and grouping them together.
- The first element on this list is called dimension reduction and the second is called clustering. Both of these are examples of unsupervised learning because they do not attempt to find a relationship between predictors and a specific response and therefore are not used to make predictions of any kind. Unsupervised models, instead, are utilized to find organizations and representations of the data that were previously unknown.

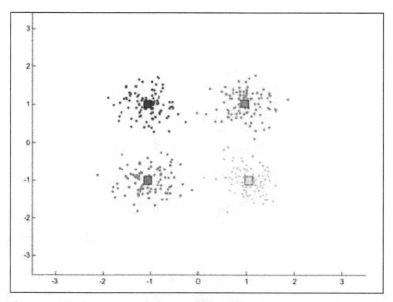

The preceding screenshot is a representation of a cluster analysis. The model will recognize that each uniquely colored cluster of observations is similar to another but different from the other clusters.

A big advantage for unsupervised learning is that it does not require labeled data, which means that it is much easier to get data that complies with unsupervised learning models. Of course, a drawback to this is that we lose all predictive power because the response variable holds the information to make predictions and without it our model will be hopeless in making any sort of predictions.

A big drawback is that it is difficult to see how well we are doing. In a regression or classification problem, we can easily tell how well our models are predicting by comparing our models' answers to the actual answers. For example, if our supervised model predicts rain and it is sunny outside, the model was incorrect.

If our supervised model predicts the price will go up by 1 dollar and it goes up by 99 cents, our model was very close! In supervised modeling, this concept is foreign because we have no answer to compare our models to. Unsupervised models are merely suggesting differences and similarities, which then requires a human's interpretation.

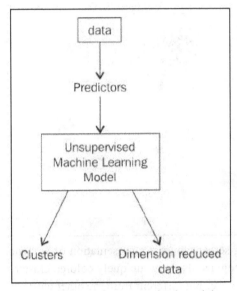

An overview of unsupervised models

In short, the main goal of unsupervised models is to find similarities and differences between data observations. We will discuss unsupervised models in depth in later chapters.

Reinforcement learning

In reinforcement learning, algorithms get to choose an action in an environment and then are rewarded (positively or negatively) for choosing this action. The algorithm then adjusts itself and modifies its strategy in order to accomplish some goal, which is usually to get more rewards.

This type of machine learning is very popular in AI-assisted game play as agents (the AI) are allowed to explore a virtual world and collect rewards and learn the best navigation techniques. This model is also popular in robotics, especially in the field of self-automated machinery, including cars:

Self-driving cars read in sensor input, act accordingly and are then rewarded for taking a certain action. The car then adjusts its behavior to collect more rewards.
Image source: https://www.quora.com/How-do-Googles-self-driving-cars-work

It can be thought that reinforcement is similar to supervised learning in that the agent is learning from its past actions to make better moves in the future; however, the main difference lies in the reward. The reward does not have to be tied in any way to a "correct" or "incorrect" decision. The reward simply encourages (or discourages) different actions.

Reinforcement learning is the least explored of the three types of machine learning and therefore is not explored in great length in this text. The remainder of the chapter will focus on supervised and unsupervised learning.

Overview of the types of machine learning

Of the three types of machine learning—supervised, unsupervised, and reinforcement learning—we can imagine the world of machine learning as something like this:

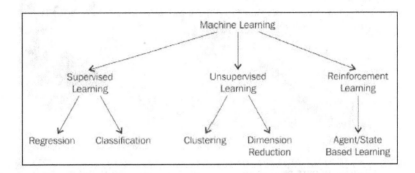

Each of the three types of machine learning has its benefits and also its drawbacks, as listed:

• Supervised machine learning: This exploits relationships between predictors and response variables to make predictions of future data observations.
Pros:
- It can make future predictions
- It can quantify relationships between predictors and response variables
- It can show us how variables affect each other and how much

Cons:
- It requires labeled data (which can be difficult to get)

• Unsupervised machine learning: This finds similarities and differences between data points.
Pros:
- It can find groups of data points that behave similarly that a human would never have noted.
- It can be a preprocessing step for supervised learning .
- Think of clustering a bunch of data points and then using these clusters as the response!.

- It can use unlabeled data, which is much easier to find.

Cons:

- It has zero predictive power
- It can be hard to determine if we are on the right track
- It relies much more on human interpretation

• Reinforcement learning: This is reward-based learning that encourages agents to take particular actions in their environments.

Pros:

- Very complicated rewards systems create very complicated AI systems.
- It can learn in almost any environment, including our own Earth.

Cons:

- The agent is erratic at first and makes many terrible choices before realizing that these choices have negative rewards.

For example, a car might crash into a wall and not know that that is not okay until the environment negatively rewards it.

- It can take a while before the agent avoids decisions altogether.
- The agent might play it safe and only choose one action and be "too afraid" to try anything else for fear of being punished.

5.5 Statistical modeling

Up until now, I have been using the term machine learning, but you may ask how statistical modeling plays a role in all of this.

This is still a debated topic in the field of data science. I believe that statistical modeling is another term for machine learning models that heavily relies on using mathematical rules borrowed from probability and statistics to create relationships between data variables (often in a predictive sense).

The remainder of this chapter will focus mostly on one statistical/probabilistic model—linear regression.

5.6 Linear regression

Finally! We will explore our first true machine learning model. Linear regressions are a form of regression, which means that it is a machine learning model that attempts to find a relationship between predictors and a response variable and that response variable is, you guessed it, continuous! This notion is synonymous with making a line of best fit.

In the case of linear regression, we will attempt to find a linear relationship between our predictors and our response variable. Formally, we wish to solve for a formula of the following format:

$$y = \beta_0 + \beta_1 x_1 + \beta_2 x_2 + \cdots + \beta_n x_n$$

- y is our response variable
- xi is our ith variable (ith column or ith predictor)
- B0 is the intercept
- Bi is the coefficient for the xi term

Let's take a look at some data before we go in-depth. This dataset is publically available and attempts to predict the number of bikes needed on a particular day for a bike sharing program:

```
# read the data and set the datetime as the index
#  taken  from  Kaggle:  https://www.kaggle.com/c/bike-sharing-
demand/data
import pandas as pd
import matplotlib.pyplot as plt
%matplotlib inline
url = 'https://raw.githubusercontent.com /justmarkham/ DAT8/master/
data/bikeshare.csv'
bikes = pd.read_csv(url)

bikes.head()
```

	datetime	season	holiday	workingday	weather	temp	atemp	humidity	windspeed	casual	registered	count
0	2011-01-01 00:00:00	1	0	0	1	9.84	14.395	81	0	3	13	16
1	2011-01-01 01:00:00	1	0	0	1	9.02	13.635	80	0	8	32	40
2	2011-01-01 02:00:00	1	0	0	1	9.02	13.635	80	0	5	27	32
3	2011-01-01 03:00:00	1	0	0	1	9.84	14.395	75	0	3	10	13
4	2011-01-01 04:00:00	1	0	0	1	9.84	14.395	75	0	0	1	1

We can see that every row represents a single hour of bike usage. In this case, we are interested in predicting count, which represents the total number of bikes rented in the period of that hour.

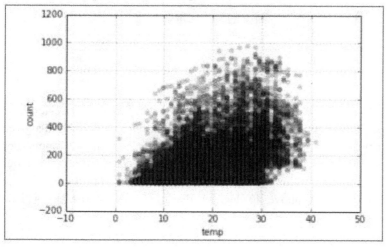

Let's, for example, look at a scatter plot between temperature (the temp column) and count, as shown:

bikes.plot(kind='scatter', x='temp', y='count', alpha=0.2)

And now, let's use a module, called seaborn, to draw ourselves a line of best fit, as follows:

import seaborn as sns #using seaborn to get a line of best fit
*sns.lmplot(x='temp', y='count', data=bikes, aspect=1.5, scatter_*
kws={'alpha':0.2})

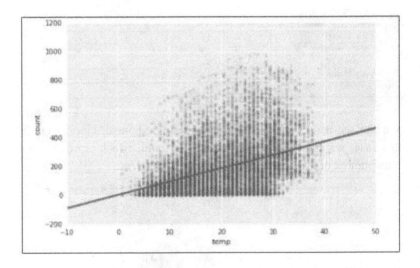

This line in the graph attempts to visualize and quantify the relationship between temp and count. To make a prediction, we simply find a given temperature, and then see where the line would predict the count. For example, if the temperature is 20 degrees (Celsius mind you), then our line would predict that about 200 bikes will be rented. If the temperature is above 40 degrees, then more than 400 bikes will be needed!

It appears that as temp goes up, our count also goes up. Let's see if our correlation value, which quantifies a linear relationship between variables, also matches this notion:

83

bikes[['count', 'temp']].corr()
 # 0.3944

There is a (weak) positive correlation between the two variables! Now, let's go back to the form of the linear regression:

$$y = \beta_0 + \beta_1 x_1 + \beta_2 x_2 + \cdots + \beta_n x_n$$

Our model will attempt to draw a perfect line between all the dots in the preceding graph, but of course, we can clearly see that there is no perfect line between these dots! The model will then find the best fit line possible. How? We can draw infinite lines between the data points, but what makes a line the best?

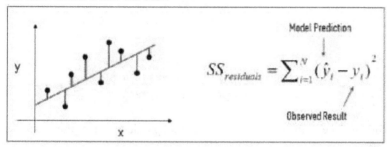

In our model, we are given the x and the y and the model learns the Beta coefficients, also known as model coefficients:

- The black dots are the observed values of x and y.
- The blue line is our line of best fit.
- The red lines between the dots and the line are called the residuals;

they are the distances between the observed values and the line. They are how wrong the line is.

Each data point has a residual, or a distance to the line of best fit. The sum of squared residuals is the summation of each residual squared. The best fit line has the smallest sum of squared residual value. Let's build this line in Python, shall we?

 # create X and y
feature_cols = ['temp'] # a lsit of the predictors
X = bikes[feature_cols] # subsetting our data to only the predictors
y = bikes['count'] # our response variable

Note how we made an X and a y variable. These represent our predictors and our response variable.

Then, we will import our machine learning module, scikit learn, as shown:

 # import scikit-learn, our machine learning module
from sklearn.linear_model import LinearRegression

Finally, we will fit our model to the predictors and the response variable, as follows:

linreg = LinearRegression() #instantiate a new model
linreg.fit(X, y) #fit the model to our data
 # print the coefficients
*print linreg.intercept_*
*print linreg.coef_*
6.04621295962 # our Beta_0
[9.17054048] # our beta parameters

To interpret:

• B0 (6.04) is the value of y when X = 0.

It is the estimation of bikes that will be rented when the temperature is 0 Celsius.

So, at 0 degrees, six bikes are predicted to be in use (its cold!).

Sometimes, it might not make sense to interpret the intercept at all because there might not be a concept of zero of something. Recall the levels of data. Not all levels have this notion. Temperature exists at a level that has the inherent notion of no bikes; so, we are safe. Be careful in the future though and always ask yourself, does it make sense to have none of this thing:

• B1 (9.17) is our temp coefficient.

   • It is the change in y divided by the change in x1.
   • It represents how x and y move together.
   • A change in 1 degree Celsius is associated with an increase of about 9 bikes rented.
   • The sign of this coefficient is important. If it were negative, that would imply that a rise in temperature is associated with a drop in rentals.

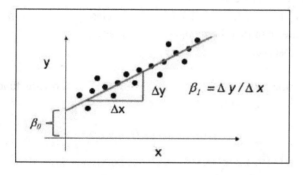

Consider the preceding representation of the Beta coefficients in a linear regression:

It is important to reiterate that these are all statements of correlation and not a statement of causation. We have no means of stating whether or not the rental increase is caused by the change in temperature, it is just that there appears to be movement together.

Using scikit-learn to make predictions is easy!

linreg.predict(20)
 # 189.4570

This means that 190 bikes will likely be rented if the temperature is 20 degrees.

5.7 Logistic regression

Our first classification model is called logistic regression. I can already hear the questions you have in your head: what makes is logistic, why is it called regression if you claim that this is a classification algorithm? All in good time, my friend.

Logistic regression is a generalization of the linear regression model adapted to fit classification problems. In linear regression, we use a set of quantitative feature variables to predict a continuous response variable. In logistic regression, we use a set of quantitative feature variables to predict probabilities of class membership. These probabilities can then be mapped to class labels, thus predicting a class for each observation.

When performing linear regression, we use the following function to make our line of best fit:

$$y = \beta_0 + \beta_1 x$$

Here, y is our response variable (the thing we wish to predict), our Beta represents our model parameters and x represents our input variable (a single one in this case, but it can take in more, as we have seen).
Briefly, let's assume that one of the response options in our classification problem is the class 1.

When performing logistic regression, we use the following form:

$$\pi = \Pr\left(y = 1 \mid x\right) = \frac{e^{\beta_0 + \beta_1 x}}{1 + e^{\beta_0 + \beta_1 x}}$$

Probability of y = 1, given x

Here, represents the conditional probability that our response variable belongs to class 1, given our data x. Now, you might be wondering what on earth is that monstrosity of a function on the right-hand side, and where did the e variable come from? Well, that monstrosity is called the logistic function, and it is actually wonderful. And that variable, e, is no variable at all. Let's back up a tick.

The variable e is a special number, like . It is, approximately, 2.718, and is called Euler's number. It is used frequently in modeling environments with natural growth and decay. For example, scientists use e in order to model the population growth of bacteria and buffalo alike. Euler's number is used to model the radioactive decay of chemicals and also to calculate continuous compound interest! Today, we will use e for a very special purpose, for machine learning.

Why can't we just make a linear regression directly to the probability of the data point belonging to a certain class like this?

$$\Pr\left(y = 1 \mid x\right) = y = \beta_0 + \beta_1 x$$

We can't do that for a few reasons, but I will point out a big one. Linear regression, because it attempts to relate to a continuous response variable, assumes that our y is continuous. In our case, y would represent the probability of an event occurring. Even though our probability is, in fact, a continuous range, it is just that—a range between 0 and 1. A line would extrapolate beyond 0 and 1 and be able to predict a probability of -4 or 1,542! We can't have that. Our graph must be bound neatly between 0 and 1 on the y axis like a real probability is.

Another reason is a bit more philosophical. Using a linear regression, we are making a serious assumption. Our big assumption here is that there is a linear relationship between probability and our features. In general, if we think about the probability of an event, we tend to think of smooth curves representing them, not a single boring line. So, we need something a bit more appropriate. For this, let us go back and revisit basic probability for a minute.

5.8 Probability, odds, and log odds

We are familiar with the basic concept of probability in that the probability of an event occurring can be simply modeled as the number of ways the event can occur divided by all the possible outcomes. For example, if, out of 3,000 people who walked into a store, 1,000 actually bought something, then we could say that the probability of a single person buying an item is as shown:

$$\Pr(buy) = \frac{1,000}{3,000} = \frac{1}{3} = 33.3\%$$

However, we also have a related concept, called odds. The odds of an outcome occurring is the ratio of the number of ways that the outcome occurs divided by every other possible outcome instead of all possible outcomes. In the same example, the odds of a person buying something would be as follows:

$$Odds(buy) = \frac{1,000}{3,000} = \frac{1}{2} = .5$$

This means that for every customer you convert, you will not convert two customers. These concepts are so related, there is even a formula to get from one to the other. We have that:

$$Odds = \frac{P}{1-P}$$

Let's check this with our example, as illustrated:

$$Odds = \frac{\frac{1}{3}}{1-\frac{1}{3}} = \frac{\frac{1}{3}}{\frac{2}{3}} = \frac{1}{2}$$

It checks out!

Let's use Python to make a table of probabilities and associated odds, as shown:

```
# create a table of probability versus odds
table = pd.DataFrame({'probability':[0.1, 0.2, 0.25, 0.5, 0.6, 0.8, 0.9]})
table['odds'] = table.probability/(1 - table.probability)
table
```

	probability	odds
0	0.10	0.111111
1	0.20	0.250000
2	0.25	0.333333
3	0.50	1.000000
4	0.60	1.500000
5	0.80	4.000000
6	0.90	9.000000

So, we see that as our probabilities increase, so do our odds, but at a much faster rate! In fact, as the probability of an event occurring nears 1, our odds will shoot off into infinity. Earlier, we said that we couldn't simply regress to probability because our line would shoot off into positive and negative infinities, predicting improper probabilities, but what if we regress to odds? Well, odds go off to positive infinity, but alas, they will merely approach 0 on the bottom, but never go below 0. Therefore, we cannot simply regress to probability, or odds. It looks like we've hit rock bottom folks!

However, wait, natural numbers and logarithms to the rescue! Think of logarithms as follows:

$$if\ 2^4 = 16\ then\ \log_2 16 = 4$$

Basically, logarithms and exponents are one and the same. We are just so used to writing exponents in the first way that we forget there is another way to write them. How about another example? If we take the logarithm of a number, we are asking the question, hey, what exponent would we need to put on this number to make it the given number?

Note that np.log automatically does all logarithms in base e, which is what we want:

np.log(10) # == 2.3025
 # meaning that e ^ 2.302 == 10

 # to prove that
2.71828**2.3025850929940459 # == 9.9999
 # e ^ log(10) == 10

Let's go ahead and add the logarithm of odds, or log-odds to our table, as follows:

 # add log-odds to the table
table['logodds'] = np.log(table.odds)
table

	probability	odds	logodds
0	0.10	0.111111	-2.197225
1	0.20	0.250000	-1.386294
2	0.25	0.333333	-1.098612
3	0.50	1.000000	0.000000
4	0.60	1.500000	0.405465
5	0.80	4.000000	1.386294
6	0.90	9.000000	2.197225

So, now every row has the probability of a single event occurring, the odds of that event occurring, and now the log-odds of that event occurring. Let's go ahead and ensure that our numbers are on the up and up. Let's choose a probability of .25, as illustrated:

prob = .25

odds = prob / (1 - prob)
odds
0.33333333

logodds = np.log(odds)
logodds
-1.09861228

It checks out! Wait, look! Our logodds variable seems to go down below zero and, in fact, logodds is not bounded above, nor is it bounded below, which means that it is a great candidate for a response variable for linear regression. In fact, this is where our story of logistic regression really begins.

The math of logistic regression

The long and short of it is that logistic regression is a linear regression between our feature, X, and the log-odds of our data belonging to a certain class that we will call true for the sake of generalization.

If p represents the probability of a data point belonging to a particular class, then logistic regression can be written as follows:

$$\log_e\left(\frac{p}{1-p}\right) = \beta_0 + \beta_1 x$$

If we rearrange our variables and solve this for p, we would get the logistic function, which takes on an S shape, where y is bounded by [0,1]:

$$p = \frac{e^{\beta_0 + \beta_1 x}}{1 + e^{\beta_0 + \beta_1 x}}$$

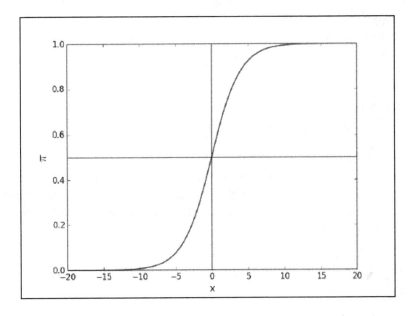

93

The preceding graph represents the logistic function's ability to map our continuous input, x, to a smooth probability curve that begins at the left, near probability 0, and as we increase x, our probability of belonging to a certain class rises naturally and smoothly up to probability 1. In other words:

- Logistic regression gives an output of the probabilities of a specific class being true
- Those probabilities can be converted into class predictions

The logistic function has some nice properties, as follows:

It takes on an S shape

- Output is bounded by 0 and 1, as a probability should be

In order to interpret the outputs of a logistic function, we must understand the difference between probability and odds. The odds of an event are given by the ratio of the probability of the event by its complement, as shown:

$$odds = \frac{p}{1-p}$$

In linear regression, parameter represents the change in the response variable for a unit change in x. In logistic regression, represents the change in the log-odds for a unit change in x. This means that e1 gives us the change in the odds for a unit change in x.

Consider that we are interested in mobile purchase behavior. Let y be a class label denoting purchase/no purchase, and let x denote whether the phone was an iPhone.

Also, suppose that we perform a logistic regression, and we get 1 = 0.693.

In this case the odds ratio is np.exp(0.693) = 2, which means that the likelihood of purchase is twice as high if the phone is an iPhone.

Dummy variables

Dummy variables are used when we are hoping to convert a categorical feature into a quantitative one. Remember that we have two types of categorical features: nominal and ordinal. Ordinal features have natural order among them, while nominal data does not.

Encoding qualitative (nominal) data using separate columns is called making dummy variables and it works by turning each unique category of a nominal column into its own column that is either true or false. For example, if we had a column for someone's college major and we wished to plug that information into a linear or logistic regression, we couldn't because they only take in numbers! So, for each row, we had new columns that represent the single nominal column. In this case, we have four unique majors: computer science, engineering, business, and literature. We end up with three new columns (we omit computer science as it is not necessary).

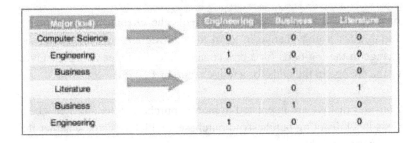

Major (bad)	Engineering	Business	Literature
Computer Science	0	0	0
Engineering	1	0	0
Business	0	1	0
Literature	0	0	1
Business	0	1	0
Engineering	1	0	0

Note that the first row has a 0 in all the columns, which means that this person did not major in engineering, did not major in business and did not major in literature. The second person has a single 1 in the engineering column as that is the major they studied.

In our bikes example, let's define a new column, called when_is_it, which is going to be one of the following four options:
- Morning
- Afternoon
- Rush_hour
- Off_hours

To do this, our approach will be to make a new column that is simply the hour of the day, use that column to determine when in the day it is, and explore whether or not we think that column might help us predict the above_daily column:

bikes['hour'] = bikes['datetime'].apply(lambda x:int(x[11]+x[12]))
 # make a column that is just the hour of the day
bikes['hour'].head()
0
1
2
3

Great, now let's define a function that turns these hours into strings. For this example, let's define the hours between 5 and 11 as morning, between 11 am and 4 pm as being afternoon, 4 and 6 as being rush hours, and everything else as being off hours:

```
# this function takes in an integer hour
# and outputs one of our four options
def when_is_it(hour):
if hour >= 5 and hour < 11:
        return "morning"
elif hour >= 11 and hour < 16:
        return "afternoon"
elif hour >= 16 and hour < 18:
        return "rush_hour"
else:
        return "off_hours"
```

Let's apply this function to our new hour column and make our brand new column,
when_is_it:

```
        bikes['when_is_it'] = bikes['hour'].apply(when_is_it)
        bikes[['when_is_it', 'above_average']].head()
```

	when_is_it	above_average
0	off_hours	False
1	off_hours	False
2	off_hours	False
3	off_hours	False
4	off_hours	False

Let's try to use only this new column to determine whether or not the hourly bike rental count will be above average. Before we do, let's do the basics of exploratory data analysis and make a graph to see if we can visualize a difference between the four times of the day. Our graph will be a bar chart with one bar per time of the day. Each bar will represent the percentage of times that this time of the day had a greater than normal bike rental:

bikes.groupby('when_is_it').above_average.mean().plot(kind='bar')

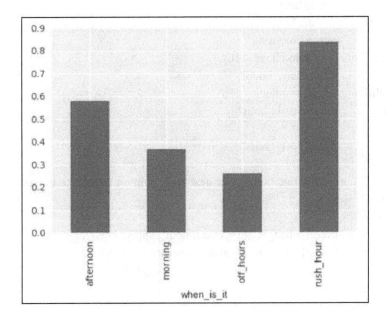

We can see that there is a pretty big difference! For example, when it is off hours, the chance of having more than average bike rentals is about 25%, whereas during rush hours, the chance of being above average is over 80%! Okay, this is exciting, but let's use some built-in Pandas tools to extract dummy columns, as follows:

*when_dummies = pd.get_dummies(bikes['when_is_it'],
prefix='when__') when_dummies.head()*

	when___afternoon	when___morning	when___off_hours	when___rush_hour
0	0.0	0.0	1.0	0.0
1	0.0	0.0	1.0	0.0
2	0.0	0.0	1.0	0.0
3	0.0	0.0	1.0	0.0
4	0.0	0.0	1.0	0.0

when_dummies = when_dummies.iloc[:, 1:]
 # remove the first column
when_dummies.head()

	when___morning	when___off_hours	when___rush_hour
0	0.0	1.0	0.0
1	0.0	1.0	0.0
2	0.0	1.0	0.0
3	0.0	1.0	0.0
4	0.0	1.0	0.0

Great! Now we have a Dataframe full of numbers that we can plug in to our logistic regression:

X = when_dummies
 # our new X is our dummy variables
y = bikes.above_average

```
logreg = LogisticRegression()
# instantate our model

logreg.fit(X_train, y_train)
# fit our model to our training set

logreg.score(X_test, y_test)
# score it on our test set to get a better sense of out of sample
performance
# 0.685157
```

Which is even better than just using the temperature! What if we tacked on temperature and humidity onto that? So, now we are using the temperature, humidity, and our time of day dummy variables to predict whether or not we will have higher than average bike rentals:

```
new_bike = pd.concat([bikes[['temp', 'humidity']], when_dummies],
axis=1)
# combine temperature, humidity, and the dummy variables

X = new_bike
# our new X is our dummy variables
y = bikes.above_average

X_train, X_test, y_train, y_test = train_test_split(X, y)

logreg = LogisticRegression()
# instantate our model

logreg.fit(X_train, y_train)
# fit our model to our training set

logreg.score(X_test, y_test)
# score it on our test set to get a better sense of out of sample
performance

# 0.7182218
```
Wow. Okay, let's quit while we're ahead.

Chapter VI
Predictions

In this chapter, we will be looking at three types of machine learning algorithms. The first two being examples of supervised learning while the final algorithm being an example of unsupervised learning.

Our goal in this chapter is to see and apply concepts learned from previous chapters in order to construct and use modern learning algorithms in order to glean insights and make predictions on real data sets. While we explore the following algorithms, we should always remember that we are constantly keeping our metrics in mind.

Let's get to it!

6.1 Naïve Bayes classification

Let's get right into it! Let's begin with Naïve Bayes classification. This machine learning model relies heavily on results from previous chapters, specifically with Bayes theorem:

$$P(H \mid D) = \frac{P(D \mid H)P(H)}{P(D)}$$

Let's look a little closer at the specific features of this formula:

- P(H) is the probability of the hypothesis before we observe the data, called the prior probability, or just prior
- P(H|D) is what we want to compute, the probability of the hypothesis after we observe the data, called the posterior
- P(D|H) is the probability of the data under the given hypothesis, called the
- likelihood
- P(D) is the probability of the data under any hypothesis, called the normalizing constant

Naïve Bayes classification is a classification model, and therefore a supervised model. Given this, what kind of data do we need?
- Labeled data
- Unlabeled data

If you answered labeled data then you're well on your way to becoming a data scientist!

Suppose we have a data set with n features, (x1, x2, ..., xn) and a class label C. For example let's take some data involving spam text classification. Our data would consist of rows of individual text samples and columns of both our features and our class labels. Our features would be words and phrases that are contained within the text samples and our class labels are simply spam or not spam. In this scenario, I will replace the class not spam with the easier to say word, ham:

import pandas as pd
import sklearn
df = pd.read_table('https://raw.githubusercontent.com/sinanuozdemir/
sfdat22/master/data/sms.tsv',

                sep='\t', header=None, names=['label', 'msg'])
df

Here is a sample of text data in a row column format:

	label	msg
0	ham	Go until jurong point, crazy.. Available only ...
1	ham	Ok lar... Joking wif u oni...
2	spam	Free entry in 2 a wkly comp to win FA Cup fina...
3	ham	U dun say so early hor... U c already then say...
4	ham	Nah I don't think he goes to usf, he lives aro...
5	spam	FreeMsg Hey there darling it's been 3 week's n...
6	ham	Even my brother is not like to speak with me. ...
7	ham	As per your request 'Melle Melle (Oru Minnamin...

Let's do some preliminary statistics to see what we are dealing with. Let's see the difference in the number of ham and spam messages at our disposal:

df.label.value_counts().plot(kind="bar")

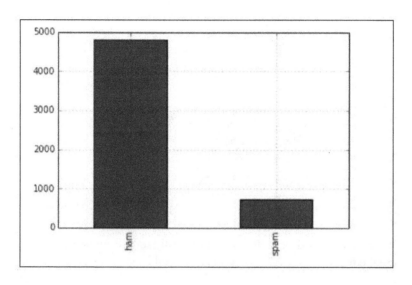

So we have WAY more ham messages than we do spam. Because this is a classification problem, it will be very useful to know our null accuracy rate which is the percentage chance of predicting a single row correctly if we keep guessing the most common class, ham:

df.label.value_counts() / df.shape[0]

ham	0.865937
spam	0.134063

So if we blindly guessed ham we would be correct about 87% of the time, but we can do better than that. If we have a set of classes, C, and a features xi, then we can use Bayes theorem to predict the probability that a single row belongs to class C using the following formula:

$$P(\text{class } C \,|\, \{x_i\}) = \frac{P(\{x_i\} \,|\, \text{class } C) \cdot P(\text{class } C)}{P(\{x_i\})}$$

Let's look at this formula in a little more detail:

- P(class C | {xi}): The posterior probability is the probability that the row belongs to class C given the features {xi}.
- P({xi} | class C): This is the likelihood that we would observe these features given that the row was in class C.
- P(class C): This is the prior probability. It is the probability that the data point belongs to class C before we see any data.
- P({xi}): This is our normalization constant.
- For example, imagine we have an e-mail with three words: send cash now. We'll use Naïve Bayes to classify the e-mail as either being spam or ham:

$$P(\text{spam} \,|\, \text{send cash now}) = P(\text{send cash now} \,|\, \text{spam}) * P(\text{spam}) / P(\text{send cash now})$$

$$P(\text{ham} \,|\, \text{send cash now}) = P(\text{send cash now} \,|\, \text{ham}) * P(\text{ham}) / P(\text{send cash now})$$

We are concerned with the difference of these two numbers. We can use the following criteria to classify any single text sample:

- If P(spam | send cash now) is larger than P(ham | send cash now), then we will classify the text as spam
- If P(ham | send cash now) is larger than P(spam | send cash now), then we will label the text as ham

Because both equations have P (send money now) on the denominator, we can ignore them.

6.2 Decision trees

Decision trees are supervised models that can either preform regression or classification.

Let's take a look at some major league baseball player data from 1986-1987. Each dot represents a single player in the league:

- Years (x axis): Number of years played in the major leagues
- Hits (y axis): Number of hits the player had in the previous year
- Salary (color): Low salary is blue/green, high salary is red/yellow

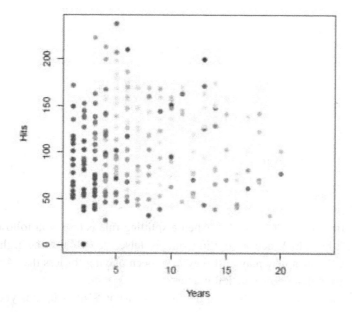

The preceding data is our training data. The idea is to build a model that predicts the salary of future players based on Years and Hits. A decision tree aims to make splits on our data in order to segment the data points that act similarly to each other, but differently to the others. The tree makes multiples of these splits in order to make the most accurate prediction possible. Let's see a tree built for the preceding data:

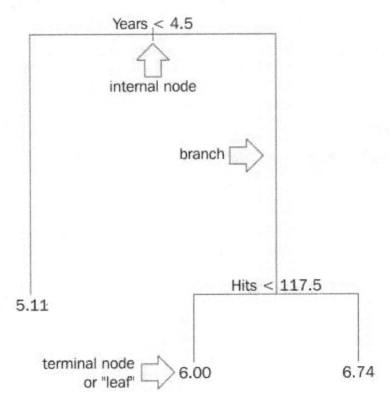

Reading from top to bottom:
• The first split is Years < 4.5, when a splitting rule is true, you follow the left branch. When a splitting rule is false, you follow the right branch. So for a new player, if they have been playing for less than 4.5 years, we will go down the left branch.
• For players in the left branch, the mean salary is $166,000, thus you label it with that value (salary has been divided by 1000 and log-transformed to 5.11 for ease of computation).
• For players in the right branch, there is a further split on Hits < 117.5, dividing players into two more salary regions: $403,000 (transformed to 6.00), and $846,000 (transformed to 6.74).

This tree doesn't just give us predictions; it also implies some more information about our data:

- It seems that the number of years in the league is the most important factor in determining salary, with a smaller number of years correlating to a lower salary
- If a player has not been playing for long (< 4.5 years), the number of hits they have is not an important factor when it comes to their salary
- For players with 5+ years under their belt, hits are an important factor for their salary determination
- Our tree only made up to two decisions before spitting out an answer (two is called our depth of the tree)

How does a computer build a regression tree?

Modern decision tree algorithms tend to use a recursive binary splitting approach:

- The process begins at the top of the tree.
- For every feature, it will examine every possible split, and choose the feature and split such that the resulting tree has the lowest possible mean squared error (MSE). The algorithm makes that split.
- It will then examine the two resulting regions, and again make a single split (in one of the regions) to minimize the MSE.
- Keep repeating step 3 until a stopping criterion is met:
    Maximum tree depth (maximum number of splits required to arrive at a leaf)
    Minimum number of observations in a leaf (final) node

For classification trees, the algorithm is very similar with the biggest difference being the metric we optimize over. Because MSE only exists for regression problems, we cannot use it. However instead of accuracy, classification trees optimize over either the gini index or entropy.

106

6.3 Unsupervised learning

It's time to see some examples of unsupervised learning, given that we spend a majority of this book on supervised learning models.

When to use unsupervised learning

There are many times when unsupervised learning can be appropriate. Some very common examples include the following:

- When there is no clear response variable. There is nothing that we are explicitly trying to predict or correlate to other variables.
- To extract structure from data where no apparent structure/patterns exist (can be a supervised learning problem).
- When an unsupervised concept called feature extraction is used. Feature extraction is the process of creating new features from existing ones. These new features can be even stronger than the original features.

The first tends to be the most common reason that data scientists choose to use unsupervised learning. This case arises frequently when we are working with data and we are not explicitly trying to predict any of the columns and we merely wish to find patterns of similar (and dissimilar) groups of points. The second option comes into play even if we are explicitly attempting to use a supervised model to predict a response variable. Sometimes simple EDA might not produce any clear patterns in the data in the few dimensions that humans can imagine where as a machine might pick up on data points behaving similarly to each other in greater dimensions.

The third common reason to use unsupervised learning is to extract new features from features that already exist. This process (lovingly called feature extraction) might produce features that can be used in a future supervised model or that can be used for presentation purposes (marketing or otherwise).

6.4 K-means clustering

K-means clustering is our first example of an unsupervised machine learning model.

Remember this means that we are not making predictions; we are trying instead to extract structure from seemingly unstructured data. Clustering is a family of unsupervised machine learning models that attempt to group data points into clusters with centroids.

The preceding definition can be quite vague, but it becomes specific when narrowed down to specific domains. For example, online shoppers who behave similarly might shop for similar things or at similar shops, whereas similar software companies might make comparable software at comparable prices.

Here is a visualization of clusters of points:

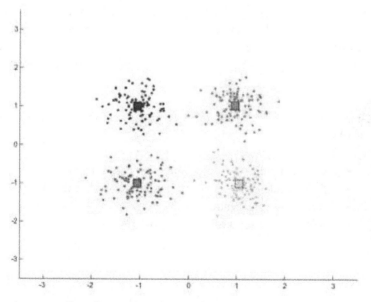

In the preceding figure, our human brains can very easily see the difference between the four clusters. Namely that the red cluster is on the bottom left of the graph while the green cluster lives in the bottom ight portion of the graph. This means that there data points are similar to each other, but not similar to data points in the other clusters.

We can also see the centroids of each cluster as the square in each color. Note that the centroid is not an actual data point, but is merely an abstraction of a cluster and represents the center of the cluster.

The concept of similarity is central to the definition of a cluster, and therefore to cluster analysis. In general, greater similarity between points leads to better clustering. In most cases, we turn data into points in n-dimensional space and use the distance between these points as a form of similarity. The centroid of the cluster then is usually the average of each dimension (column) for each data point in each cluster. So for example, the centroid of the red cluster is the result of taking the average value of each column of each red data point.

The purpose of cluster analysis is to enhance our understanding of a dataset by dividing the data into groups. Clustering provides a layer of abstraction from individual data points. The goal is to extract and enhance the natural structure of the data. There are many kinds of classification procedures. For our class, we will be focusing on K-means clustering, which is one of the most popular clustering algorithms.

K-means is an iterative method that partitions a data set into k clusters. It works in four steps:

- Choose k initial centroids (note that k is an input).
- For each point assign the point to the nearest centroid.
- Recalculate the centroid positions.
- Repeat steps 2-3 until stopping criteria is met.

6.5 Choosing an optimal number for K and cluster validation

A big part of K-means clustering is knowing the optimal number of clusters. If we knew this number ahead of time, then that might defeat the purpose of even using unsupervised learning. So we need a way to evaluate the output of our cluster analysis.

The problem here is that because we are not performing any kind of prediction, we cannot gauge how right the algorithm is at predictions. Metrics such as accuracy and RMSE go right out of the window.

The Silhouette Coefficient the Silhouette

Coefficient is a common metric for evaluating clustering performance in situations when the true cluster assignments are not known. A Silhouette Coefficient is calculated for each observation as follows:

$$SC = \frac{b - a}{\max(a, b)}$$

Let's look a little closer at the specific features of this formula:
- a: Mean distance to all other points in its cluster
- b: Mean distance to all other points in the next nearest cluster

It ranges from -1 (worst) to 1 (best). A global score is calculated by taking the mean score for all observations. In general, a silhouette coefficient of 1 is preferred, while a score of -1 is not preferable:

```
# calculate Silhouette Coefficient for K=3
from sklearn import metrics
metrics.silhouette_score(X, km.labels_)
0.4578
```

Let's try calculating the coefficient for multiple values of K to find the best value:

```
# calculate SC for K=2 through K=19
k_range = range(2, 20)
scores = []
for k in k_range:
        km = KMeans(n_clusters=k, random_state=1)
        km.fit(X_scaled)
        scores.append(metrics.silhouette_score(X, km.labels_))

# plot the results
plt.plot(k_range, scores)
plt.xlabel('Number of clusters')
plt.ylabel('Silhouette Coefficient')
plt.grid(True)
```

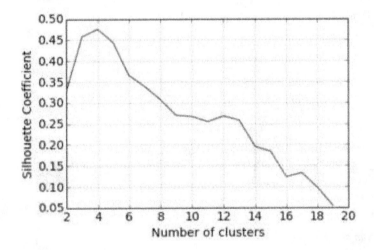

So it looks like our optimal number of beer clusters is 4! This means that our k-means algorithm has determined that there seems to be four distinct types of beer.

K-means is a popular algorithm because of its computational efficiency and simple and intuitive nature. K-means, however, is highly scale dependent, and is not suitable for data with widely varying shapes and densities. There are ways to combat this issue by scaling data using scikit-learn's standard scalar:

 # center and scale the data
from sklearn.preprocessing import StandardScaler
scaler = StandardScaler()
X_scaled = scaler.fit_transform(X)

 # K-means with 3 clusters on scaled data
km = KMeans(n_clusters=3, random_state=1)
km.fit(X_scaled)

Easy!

Now let's take a look at the third reason to use unsupervised methods that falls under the third option in our reasons to use unsupervised methods, feature extraction.

6.6 Feature extraction

Sometimes we have an overwhelming number of columns and likely not enough rows to handle the great quantity of columns.

A great example of this is when we were looking at the send cash now example in our Naïve Bayes example. We had literally 0 instances of texts with that exact phrase, so instead we turned to a naïve assumption that allowed us to extrapolate a probability for both of our categories.

The reason we had this problem in the first place is because of something called the curse of dimensionality.

The curse of dimensionality basically says that as we introduce and consider new feature columns, we need almost exponentially more rows (data points) in order to fill in the empty spaces that we create.
Consider an example where we attempt to use a learning model that utilizes the distance between points on a corpus of text that has 4,086 pieces of text, and that the whole thing has been Countvectorized. Let's assume that these texts between them have 18,884 words:

X.shape
(4086, 18884)

Now let's do an experiment. I will first consider a single word as the only dimension of our text. Then I will count how many of pieces of text are within 1 unit of each other. For example, if two sentences both contain that word, they would be 0 units away and similarly if neither of them contain the word, they would be 0 units away from one another:

d = 1
 # Let's look for points within 1 unit of one another

X_first_word = X[:,:1]
 # Only looking at the first column, but ALL of the rows

from sklearn.neighbors import NearestNeighbors
 # this module will calculate for us distances between each point

neigh = NearestNeighbors(n_neighbors=4086)
neigh.fit(X_first_word)

 # tell the module to calculate each distance between each point
A = neigh.kneighbors_graph(X_first_word, mode='distance').todense()

 # This matrix holds all distances (over 16 million of them)
num_points_within_d = (A < d).sum()

 # Count the number of pairs of points within 1 unit of distance
num_points_within_d
16258504

So 16.2 million pairs of texts are within a single unit of distance. Now let's try again with the first two words:

X_first_two_words = X[:,:2]
neigh = NearestNeighbors(n_neighbors=4086)
neigh.fit(X_first_two_words)

A = neigh.kneighbors_graph(X_first_two_words, mode='distance').
todense()

num_points_within_d = (A < d).sum()

num_points_within_d
16161970

Great! By adding this new column, we lost about 100,000 pairs of points that were within a single unit of distance. This is because we are adding space in between them for every dimension that we add. Let's take this test a step further and calculate this number for the first 100 words and then plot the results:

d = 1
 # Scan for points within one unit

num_columns = range(1, 100)
 # Looking at the first 100 columns
points = []
 # We will be collecting the number of points within 1 unit for a graph

neigh = NearestNeighbors(n_neighbors=X.shape[0])
for subset in num_columns:
X_subset = X[:,:subset]
 # look at the first column, then first two columns, then first three
columns, etc
neigh.fit(X_subset)
A = neigh.kneighbors_graph(X_subset, mode='distance').todense()
num_points_within_d = (A < d).sum()
 # calculate the number of points within 1 unit
points.append(num_points_within_d)

Now let's plot the number of points within 1 unit versus the number of dimensions we looked at:

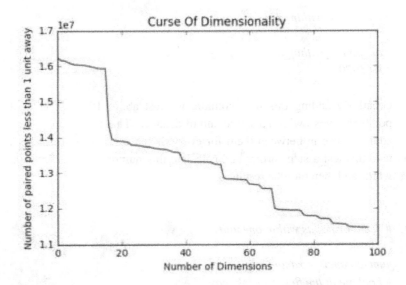

We can see clearly that the number of points within a single unit of one another goes down dramatically as we introduce more and more columns. And this is only the first 100 columns! Let's see how many points are within a single unit by the time we consider all 18,000+ words:

```
neigh = NearestNeighbors(n_neighbors=4086)
neigh.fit(X)
A = neigh.kneighbors_graph(X, mode='distance').todense()
num_points_within_d = (A < d).sum()

num_points_within_d
4090
```

By the end, only 4,000 sentences are within a unit of one another. All of this space that we add in by considering new columns makes it harder for the finite amount of points we have to stay happily within range of each other. We would have to add in more points in order to fill in this gap. And that, my friends, is why we should consider using dimension reduction.

The curse of dimensionality is solved by either adding more data points (which is not always possible), or implementing dimension reduction. Dimension reduction is simply the act of reducing the number of columns in our data set and not the number of rows. There are two ways of implementing dimension reduction:

• Feature selection: This is the act of subsetting our column features and only using the best features
• Feature extraction: This is the act of mathematically transforming our feature set into a new extracted coordinate system

We are familiar with feature selection as the process of saying the Emabrked_Q is not helping my decision tree; let's get rid of it and see how it performs. It is literally when we (or the machine) make the decision to ignore certain columns.

Feature extraction is a bit trickier...

In feature extraction, we are using usually fairly complicated mathematical formulas in order to obtain new super-columns that are usually better than any single original column.

Our primary model for doing so is called Principal Component Analysis (PCA).
PCA will extract a set number of super-columns in order to represent our original data with much fewer columns. Let's take a concrete example. Previously I mentioned some text with 4,086 rows and over 18,000 columns. That dataset is actually a set of Yelp online reviews:

```
url = '../data/yelp.csv'
yelp = pd.read_csv(url, encoding='unicode-escape')
# create a new DataFrame that only contains the 5-star and 1-star
reviews
yelp_best_worst = yelp[(yelp.stars==5) | (yelp.stars==1)]
# define X and y
```

```
X = yelp_best_worst.text
y = yelp_best_worst.stars == 5
```

Our goal is to predict whether or not a person gave a 5 or 1 star review based on the words they used in the review. Let's set a base line with logistic regression and see how well we can predict this binary category:

```
from sklearn.linear_model import LogisticRegression
lr = LogisticRegression()
X_train, X_test, y_train, y_test = train_test_split(X, y, random_state=100)

# Make our training and testing sets
vect = CountVectorizer(stop_words='english')
# Count the number of words but remove stop words like a, an, the, you, etc
X_train_dtm = vect.fit_transform(X_train)
X_test_dtm = vect.transform(X_test)
# transform our text into document term matrices
lr.fit(X_train_dtm, y_train)
# fit to our training set
lr.score(X_test_dtm, y_test)
# score on our testing set
0.91193737
```

So by utilizing all of the words in our corpus, our model seems to have over a 91% accuracy. Not bad!

Let's try only using the top 100 used words:

```
vect = CountVectorizer(stop_words='english', max_features=100)
# Only use the 100 most used words
X_train_dtm = vect.fit_transform(X_train)
X_test_dtm = vect.transform(X_test)
print X_test_dtm.shape # (1022, 100)
lr.fit(X_train_dtm, y_train)
lr.score(X_test_dtm, y_test)
```

0.8816

Note how our training and testing matrices have 100 columns. This is because I told our vectorizer to only look at the top 100 words. See also that our performance took a hit and is now down to 88% accuracy. This makes sense because we are ignoring over 4,700 words in our corpus.

6.7 K folds cross-validation

K folds cross-validation is a much better estimator of our model's performance, even more so than our train-test split. Here's how it works:

- We will take a finite number of equal slices of our data (usually 3, 5, or 10).
- Assume that this number is called k.
- For each "fold" of the cross-validation, we will treat k-1 of the sections as the training set, and the remaining section as our test set.
- For the remaining folds, a different arrangement of k-1 sections is considered for our training set and a different section is our training set.
- We compute a set metric for each fold of the cross-validation.
- We average our scores at the end.

Cross-validation is effectively using multiple train-test splits being done on the same dataset. This is done for a few reasons, but mainly because cross-validation is the most honest estimate of our model's out of the sample error.

To explain this visually, let's look at our mammal brain and body weight example for a second. The following code manually creates a five-fold cross-validation, wherein five different training and test sets are made from the same population:

```
from sklearn.cross_validation import KFold
df = pd.read_table('http://people.sc.fsu.edu/~jburkardt/
datasets/regression/x01.txt', sep='\s+', skiprows=33,
```

```
names=['id','brain','body'])
df = df[df.brain < 300][df.body < 500]
# limit points for visibility
nfolds = 5
fig, axes = plt.subplots(1, nfolds, figsize=(14,4))
for i, fold in enumerate(KFold(len(df), n_folds=nfolds,
shuffle=True)):
training, validation = fold
x, y = df.iloc[training]['body'], df.iloc[training]['brain']
axes[i].plot(x, y, 'ro')
x, y = df.iloc[validation]['body'], df.iloc[validation]['brain']
axes[i].plot(x, y, 'bo')
plt.tight_layout()
```

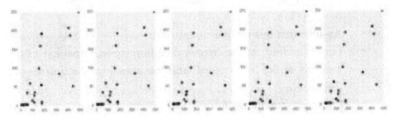

Five-fold cross-validation: red = training sets, blue = test sets

Here, each graph shows the exact same population of mammals, but the
dots are colored red if they belong to the training set of that fold and
blue if they belong to the testing set. By doing this, we are obtaining
five different instances of the same machine learning model in order to
see if performance remains consistent across the folds.

If you stare at the dots long enough, you will note that each dot appears
in a training set exactly four times (k − 1), while the same dot appears
in a test set exactly once and only once.

Some features of K-fold cross-validation include the following:

- It is a more accurate estimate of the OOS prediction error than
  a single train-test split because it is taking several independent
  train-test splits and averaging the results together.

119

- It is a more efficient use of data than single train-test splits because the entire dataset is being used for multiple train-test splits instead of just one.
- Each record in our dataset is used for both training and testing.
- This method presents a clear tradeoff between efficiency and computational expense. A 10-fold CV is 10x more expensive computationally than a single train/test split.
- This method can be used for parameter tuning and model selection.

Basically, whenever we wish to test a model on a set of data, whether we just completed tuning some parameters or feature engineering, a k-fold cross-validation is an excellent way to estimate the performance on our model. Of course, sklearn comes with an easier-to-use cross-validation module, called cross_val_score, which automatically splits up our dataset for us, runs the model on each fold, and gives us a neat and tidy output of results:

```
# Using a training set and test set is so important
# Just as important is cross validation. Remember cross validation
# is using several different train test splits and
# averaging your results!

## CROSS-VALIDATION

# check CV score for K=1
from sklearn.cross_validation import cross_val_score, train_test_split
tree = KNeighborsClassifier(n_neighbors=1)
scores = cross_val_score(tree, X, y, cv=5, scoring='accuracy')
scores.mean()
0.95999999999
```

Which is a much more reasonable accuracy than our previous score of 1. Remember that we are not getting 100% accuracy anymore, because we have a distinct training and test set. The data points that KNN has never seen the test points and therefore cannot match them exactly to themselves.

Let's try cross-validating KNN with K=5 (increasing our model's complexity), as shown:

```
# check CV score for K=5
knn = KNeighborsClassifier(n_neighbors=5)
scores = cross_val_score(knn, X, y, cv=5, scoring='accuracy')
scores
np.mean(scores)
0.97333333
```

Even better! So, now we have to find the best K? The best K is the one that maximizes our accuracy. Let's try a few:

```
# search for an optimal value of K
k_range = range(1, 30, 2) # [1, 3, 5, 7, ..., 27, 29]
errors = []
for k in k_range:
knn = KNeighborsClassifier(n_neighbors=k)
# instantiate a KNN with k neighbors
scores = cross_val_score(knn, X, y, cv=5, scoring='accuracy')
# get our five accuracy scores
accuracy = np.mean(scores)
# average them together
error = 1 – accuracy
# get our error, which is 1 minus the accuracy
errors.append(error)
# keep track of a list of errors
```

We now have an error value (1 – accuracy) for each value of K (1, 3, 5, 7, 9.., .., 29):
```
# plot the K values (x-axis) versus the 5-fold CV score (y-axis)
plt.figure()
plt.plot(k_range, errors)
plt.xlabel('K')
plt.ylabel('Error')
```

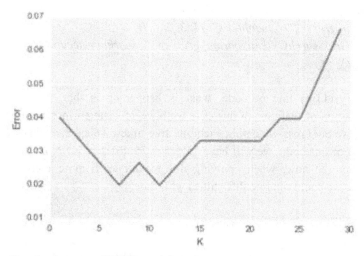

Graph of errors of KNN model against KNN's complexity, represented by the value of K

Compare this graph to the previous graph of model complexity and bias/variance. Toward the left, our graph has a higher bias and is underfitting. As we increased our model's complexity, the error term began to go down, but after a while, our model became overly complex, and the high variance kicked in, making our error term go back up.
It seems that the optimal value of K is between 6 and 10.

6.8 Grid searching

Sklearn also has, up its sleeve, another useful tool called grid searching. A grid search will by brute force try many different model parameters and give us the best one based on a metric of our choosing. For example, we can choose to optimize KNN for accuracy in the following manner:

```
from sklearn.grid_search import GridSearchCV
# import our grid search module
knn = KNeighborsClassifier()
# instantiate a blank slate KNN, no neighbors
k_range = range(1, 30, 2)
```

```
param_grid = dict(n_neighbors=k_range)
# param_grid = {"n_ neighbors": [1, 3, 5, ...]}
grid = GridSearchCV(knn, param_grid, cv=5, scoring='accuracy')
grid.fit(X, y)
```

In the grid.fit() line of code, what is happening is that, for each combination of features, in this case we have 15 different possibilities for K, we are cross-validating each one five times. This means that by the end of this code, we will have 15 * 5 = 75 different KNN models! You can see how, when applying this technique to more complex models, we could run into difficulties with time:

```
# check the results of the grid search
grid.grid_scores_
grid_mean_scores = [result[1] for result in grid.grid_scores_]
# this is a list of the average accuracies for each parameter
# combination
plt.figure()
plt.ylim([0.9, 1])
plt.xlabel('Tuning Parameter: N nearest neighbors')
plt.ylabel('Classification Accuracy')
plt.plot(k_range, grid_mean_scores)

plt.plot(grid.best_params_['n_neighbors'], grid.best_score_, 'ro',
markersize=12, markeredgewidth=1.5,
markerfacecolor='None', markeredgecolor='r')
```

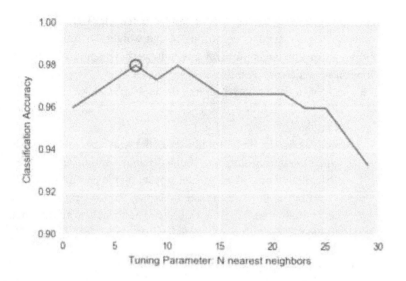

Note that the preceding graph is basically the same as the one we achieved previously with our for loop, but much easier!

We see that seven neighbors (circled in the preceding graph) seem to have the best accuracy. However, we can also, very easily, get our best parameters and our best model, as shown:

*grid.best_params_*
 # {'n_neighbors': 7}

*grid.best_score_*
 # 0.9799999999

*grid.best_estimator_*
 # actually returns the unfit model with the best parameters
 # KNeighborsClassifier(algorithm='auto', leaf_size=30, metric='minkowski',
*   metric_params=None, n_jobs=1, n_neighbors=7, p=2,*
*   weights='uniform')*

I'll take this one step further. Maybe you've noted that KNN has other parameters as well, such as algorithm, p, and weights. A quick look at the scikit-learn documentation reveals that we have some options for each of these, which are as follows:

- p is an integer and represents the type of distance we wish to use. By default, we use p=2, which is our standard distance formula.
- Weights is, by default, uniform, but can also be distance, which weighs points by their distance, which means that closer neighbors have a greater impact on the prediction.
- Algorithm is how the model finds the nearest neighbors. We can try ball_tree, kd_tree, or brute. The default is auto, which tries to use the best one automatically.

```
knn = KNeighborsClassifier()
k_range = range(1, 30)
algorithm_options = ['kd_tree', 'ball_tree', 'auto', 'brute']
p_range = range(1, 8)
weight_range = ['uniform', 'distance']
param_grid = dict(n_neighbors=k_range, weights=weight_range,
algorithm=algorithm_options, p=p_range)
# trying many more options
grid = GridSearchCV(knn, param_grid, cv=5, scoring='accuracy')
grid.fit(X, y)
```

The preceding code takes about a minute to run on my laptop because it is trying many, 1, 648, different combinations of parameters and cross-validating each one five times. All in all, to get the best answer, it is fitting 8,400 different KNN models!

```
grid.best_score_
0.98666666
```

```
grid.best_params_
{'algorithm': 'kd_tree', 'n_neighbors': 6, 'p': 3, 'weights':
'uniform'}
```

Grid searching is a simple (but inefficient) way of parameter tuning our models to get the best possible outcome. It should be noted that to get the best possible outcome, data scientists should use feature manipulation (both reduction and engineering) to obtain better results in practice as well. It should not merely be up to the model to achieve the best performance.

6.9 Ensembling techniques

Ensemble learning, or ensembling, is the process of combining multiple predictive models to produce a supermodel that is more accurate than any individual model on its own.

- **Regression:** We will take the average of the predictions for each model
- **Classification:** Take a vote and use the most common prediction, or take the average of the predicted probabilities

Imagine that we are working on a binary classification problem (predicting either 0 or 1).

ENSEMBLING

import numpy as np

 # set a seed for reproducibility
np.random.seed(12345)

 # generate 1000 random numbers (between 0 and 1) for each model,
representing 1000 observations
mod1 = np.random.rand(1000)
mod2 = np.random.rand(1000)
mod3 = np.random.rand(1000)
mod4 = np.random.rand(1000)
mod5 = np.random.rand(1000)

Now, we simulate five different learning models that each have about a 70% accuracy, as follows:

```
# each model independently predicts 1 (the "correct response") if
random number was at least 0.3
preds1 = np.where(mod1 > 0.3, 1, 0)
preds2 = np.where(mod2 > 0.3, 1, 0)
preds3 = np.where(mod3 > 0.3, 1, 0)
preds4 = np.where(mod4 > 0.3, 1, 0)

preds5 = np.where(mod5 > 0.3, 1, 0)

print preds1.mean()
0.699
print preds2.mean()
0.698
print preds3.mean()
0.71
print preds4.mean()
0.699
print preds5.mean()
0.685

# Each model has an "accuracy of around 70% on its own
```

Now, let's apply my degrees in magic. Er sorry, math.

```
# average the predictions and then round to 0 or 1
ensemble_preds = np.round((preds1 + preds2 + preds3 + preds4 +
preds5)/5.0).astype(int)
ensemble_preds.mean()

0.83
```

As you add more models to a voting process, the probability of errors will decrease; this is known as Condorcet's jury theorem.

Crazy, right?

For ensembling to work well in practice, the models must have the following characteristics:

- Accuracy: Each model must at least outperform the null model
- Independence: A model's prediction is not affected by another model's prediction process

If you have a bunch of individually OK models, the edge case mistakes made by one model are probably not going to be made by the other models, so the mistakes will be ignored when combining the models.

There are the following two basic methods for ensembling:

- Manually ensemble your individual models by writing a good deal of code
- Use a model that ensembles for you

We're going to look at a model those ensembles for us. To do this, let's take a look at decision trees again. Decision trees tend to have low bias and high variance. Given any dataset, the tree can keep asking questions (making decisions) until it is able to nitpick and distinguish between every single example in the dataset. It could keep asking question after question until there is only a single example in each leaf (terminal) node. The tree is trying too hard, growing too deep, and just memorizing every single detail of our training set. However, if we started over, the tree could potentially ask different questions and still grow very deep. This means that there are many possible trees that could distinguish between all elements, which means higher variance. It is unable to generalize well.

In order to reduce the variance of a single tree, we can place a restriction on the number of questions asked in a tree (the max_depth parameter) or we can create an ensemble version of decision trees, called Random forests.

6.10 Neural networks

Probably one of the most talked about machine learning models, neural networks are computational networks built to model animals' nervous systems. Before getting too deep into the structure, let's take a look at the big advantages of neural networks.

The key component of neural networks is that it is not only a complex structure, it is a complex and flexible structure. This means the following two things:

• Neural networks are able to estimate any function shape (this is called being non-parametric)
• Neural networks can adapt and literally change their own internal structure based on their environment

Basic structure

Neural networks are made up of interconnected nodes (perceptrons) that each take in input (quantitative value), and output other quantitative values. Signals travel through the network and eventually end up at a prediction node.

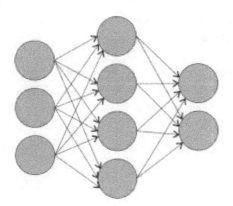

Visualization of neural network interconnected nodes

129

Another huge advantage of neural networks is that they can be used for supervised learning, unsupervised learning, and reinforcement learning problems. The ability to be so flexible, predict many functional shapes, and adapt to their surroundings make neural networks highly preferable in select fields, as follows:

- Pattern recognition: This is probably the most common application of neural networks. Some examples are handwriting recognition and image processing (facial recognition).
- Entity movement: Examples for this include self-driving cars, robotic animals, and drone movement.
- Anomaly detection: As neural networks are good at recognizing patterns, they can also be used to recognize when a data point does not fit a pattern.

Think of a neural network monitoring a stock price movement; after a while of learning the general pattern of a stock price, the network can alert you when something is unusual in the movement.

The simplest form of a neural network is a single perceptron. A perceptron, visualized as follows, takes in some input and outputs a signal:

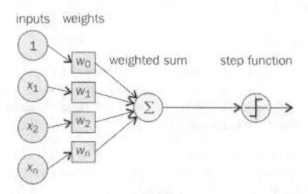

This signal is obtained by combining the input with several weights and then is put through some activation function. In cases of simple binary outputs, we generally use the logistic function, as shown:

$$f_{log}(z) = \frac{1}{1 + e^{-z}}$$

f_{log} is called logistic function

To create a neural network, we need to connect multiple perceptrons to each other in a network fashion, as illustrated in the following graph.

A multilayer perceptrons (MLP) is a finite acyclic graph. The nodes are neurons with logistic activation.

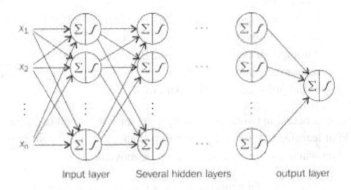

Input layer   Several hidden layers   output layer

As we train the model, we update the weights (which are random at first) of the model in order to get the best predictions possible. If an observation goes through the model and is outputted as false when it should have been true, the logistic functions in the single perceptrons are changed slightly. This is called backpropagation.

Neural networks are usually trained in batches, which means that the network is given several training data points at once several times, and each time, the back-propagation algorithm will trigger an internal weight change in the network.

It isn't hard to see that we can grow the network very deep and have many hidden layers, which are associated to the complexity of the neural network. When we grow our neural networks very deep, we are dipping our toes into the idea of deep learning.

The main advantage of deep neural networks (networks with many layers) is that they can approximate almost any shape function and they

131

can (theoretically) learn optimal combinations of features for us and use these combinations to obtain the best predictive power.

Let's see it in action. I will be using a module, called PyBrain, to make my neural networks. However, first, let's take a look at a new dataset, which is a dataset of handwritten digits. We will first try to recognize digits using a Random forest, as shown:

from sklearn.cross_validation import cross_val_score

from sklearn import datasets

import matplotlib.pyplot as plt

from sklearn.ensemble import RandomForestClassifier

%matplotlib inline

digits = datasets.load_digits()

plt.imshow(digits.images[100], cmap=plt.cm.gray_r,

interpolation='nearest')

 # a 4 digit

```
X, y = digits.data, digits.target

# 64 pixels per image

X[0].shape

# Try Random Forest

rfclf = RandomForestClassifier(n_estimators=100, random_state=1)

cross_val_score(rfclf, X, y, cv=5, scoring='accuracy').mean()

0.9382782
```

Pretty good! An accuracy of 94% is nothing to laugh at, but can we do even better?

```
# pybrain has its own data sample class that we must add

# our training and test set to

ds = ClassificationDataSet(64, 1 , nb_classes=10)

for k in xrange(len(X)):

ds.addSample(ravel(X[k]),y[k])

# their equivalent of train test split

test_data, training_data = ds.splitWithProportion( 0.25 )

# pybrain's version of dummy variables

test_data._convertToOneOfMany( )

training_data._convertToOneOfMany( )

print test_data.indim # number of pixels going in

# 64

print test_data.outdim # number of possible options (10 digits)
```

 # 10

 # instantiate the model with 64 hidden layers (standard params)

fnn = buildNetwork(training_data.indim, 64, training_data.outdim,

outclass=SoftmaxLayer)

trainer = BackpropTrainer(fnn, dataset=training_data, momentum=0.1,

learningrate=0.01 , verbose=True, weightdecay=0.01)

 # change the number of epochs to try to get better results!

trainer.trainEpochs (10) # 10 batches

*print 'Percent Error on Test dataset: ', *

percentError(trainer.testOnClassData (

dataset=test_data)

, test_data['class'])

The model will output a final error on a test set:

Percent Error on Test dataset: 4.67706013363

accuracy = 1 - .0467706013363

accuracy

0.95322

Already better! Both the random forests and neural networks do very well with this problem because both of them are non-parametric, which means that they do not rely on the underlying shape of data to make predictions. They are able to estimate any shape of function.

To predict the shape, we can use the following code:

plt.imshow(digits.images[0], cmap=plt.cm.gray_r,

interpolation='nearest')

fnn.activate(X[0])

array([0.92183643, 0.00126609, 0.00303146, 0.00387049,

0.01067609,

0.00718017, 0.00825521, 0.00917995, 0.00696929,

0.02773482])

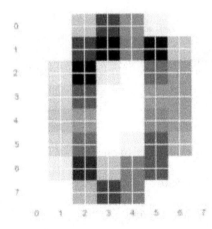

The array represents a probability for every single digit, which means that there is a 92% chance that the digit in the preceding screenshot is a 0 (which it is). Note how the next highest probability is for a 9, which makes sense because 9 and 0 have similar shapes (ovular).

Neural networks do have a major flaw. If left alone, they have a very high variance.

To see this, let's run the exact same code as the preceding one and train the exact same type of neural network on the exact same data, as illustrated:

Do it again and see the difference in error

fnn = buildNetwork(training_data.indim, 64, training_data.outdim,

outclass=SoftmaxLayer)

trainer   =   BackpropTrainer(fnn, dataset=training_data, momentum=0.1,

learningrate=0.01 , verbose=True, weightdecay=0.01)

change the number of eopchs to try to get better results!

trainer.trainEpochs (10)

print 'Percent Error on Test dataset: ' , \

percentError(trainer.testOnClassData (

dataset=test_data)

, test_data['class'])

accuracy = 1 - .0645879732739

accuracy

0.93541

See how just rerunning the model and instantiating different weights made the network turn out to be different than before? This is a symptom of being a high variance model. In addition, neural networks generally require many training samples in order to combat the high varianceness of the model and also require a large amount of computation power to work well in production environments.

www.ingramcontent.com/pod-product-compliance
Lightning Source LLC
Chambersburg PA
CBHW071251050326
40690CB00011B/2353